BUILDING BELONGING

Your Guide to Starting a
Residential Intentional Community

Yana Ludwig

Also by Yana Ludwig:

Together Resilient: Building Community in the Age of Climate Disruption
(under the name Maikwe Ludwig)

The Cooperative Culture Handbook: A Social Change Manual to Dismantle Toxic Culture and Build Connection: 26 Keys for Groups, Facilitators, Leaders, and Other Change Catalysts
Co-authored with Karen Gimnig

This book and others by the author may be ordered at:
www.ic.org/community-bookstore

This book is dedicated to

Kara Massie, who died five days before Solidarity Collective found our property,
and thus narrowly missed the chance to live the dream she helped envision

and

Tizita Assefa, who represents the most loving and
discerning of community dreamers in my life

and

Almut Zieher, whose community journey has been intermingling with mine for years,
and whose love and support literally made my last community start possible

Building Belonging:
Your Guide to Starting a Residential Intentional Community

By Yana Ludwig

ACKNOWLEDGEMENTS

Deep gratitude to the Board and staff of the Foundation for Intentional Community for once again publishing a bunch of my words. Special thanks to Kim Kanney for essentially being our project manager and lovingly holding this project (and me) at every stage; to Sky Blue for being an enduring influence and friend for me, FIC, and the movement; to Lauren Hugel for organizing events and courses to help this material develop; and to the whole Communications Team for helping make sure this is really an FIC book, and not *just* a bunch of my words.

Cassandra Ferrera worked on the earliest draft with me, and her influence is lightly woven through the book. Working with Cass is always a combination of gentle challenge and deep modeling of how to do all the things authentically.

Crystal Byrd Farmer once again supported my work (and me) being better by doing a read through from the lens of social justice, her insights into both race and disability issues in particular were invaluable. Clifford Paulin and Matt Stannard both read and made suggestions on the legal chapter. It's a better book because they were willing to make it so. That said, I'm still learning, and any mistakes in these areas are mine.

Harvey Baker and Matt Stannard also provided sidebar material for two very different but important topics: Fair Housing Law and trauma. Thanks for knowing more and being more articulate than me on these two topics.

Thanks as well to Dale Rudesil, Kath Faith and Raines Cohen for their consistent and generous support. These three are always there cheering me on and asking, "What do you need?" and then helping that happen. Nancy Simmers similarly deserves a shout out for being some mix of elder sister and compassionate sounding board every time I have the chance to work with her community. It's weird and lovely to have fans, and you are some of the best.

The first major draft of this book was done while I was in a writers' residency at the Rockvale Writers' Colony in Tennessee in 2021. Thanks to RWC for granting me the time and space to focus on just being a writer for a couple weeks.

Marqis Rotenberg and Jibran Ludwig deserve credit for getting me into community in the first place. Jibran continues to be a force helping me hone my thinking and not take myself (or this thing called "intentional community") so seriously that I miss being a good advocate for change.

Every community I've lived in has taught me what to do — and not do — in some significant way. Thanks to the founders (and the members who shared time and space with me while we lived with our/their decisions) of: Joy House, the Minis Kitigan Drum, East Wind Community, the Sarvis Point Avatar Community, Dancing Rabbit Ecovillage, October Sky, Sol Space, Zialua Ecovillage, and especially my comrades at Solidarity Collective where the lessons finally started to form into a coherent set of thoughts and practices.

Matt Stannard continues to be the best partner ever, both in life and community. Teaming up with Matt on this project in a more formal way was amazing. Thanks love.

BUILDING BELONGING

PART 3: TRANSITIONING TO COMMUNITY LIFE

CONCLUSION

PART 1: SETTING THE STAGE

Living in community is an inherently radical act. We're relearning how to think and relate as "we" in a culture of endemic individuality, which is a cornerstone to the global systems of oppression and exploitation that are driving us to the brink. The questions of applicability, accessibility, replicability, and scalability have to be addressed at some point, and we have to understand the depth and scope of what we're dealing with.[1]

— Sky Blue, former Executive Director
Foundation for Intentional Community

INTRODUCTION: WHAT TIME IS IT?

Every movement comes out of a particular moment in history: they are context-specific. Cooperatives emerged from horrifying conditions of the working poor in the UK in the late 1800s as people started organizing for economic control over their lives. The scientific revolution was a response to a need for objective measurement to counteract the religious fervor of the day. The civil rights movement and Black Lives Matter have taken the form they have because racism is still a prominent feature in our systems. Movements form in response to deep and timely needs.

Intentional community is in part a response to the loss of extended family structures as the norm (at least among white and middle class families), and the demise of the village. Modern mobility has allowed us to explore the whole world, but has also meant that people can choose to move away from their places of birth and never come back. There are a hundred wonderful things about that. But what all of this means is that community can no longer be taken for granted. If we want it, we have to work to create it in our lives.

As we have lost community to the culture of hyper-individualism and competition, many of us find ourselves longing for deeper human connections. So what time is it? What is the historical moment we find ourselves in and why must intentional communities play a role in it?

There's a lot to answering that question.

More than ever before in the US, there is a call for reckoning with our racialized, colonial status quo. Climate disruption is now killing and displacing millions of people every

---

1   In Community, On the Road, Dispatch #4, Jackson, MS, Posted on ic.org March 23, 2019.

year, and individuals and communities are scrambling to know what to do with such an unprecedented, universally impactful ecological crisis. Economic disparities within the US (as well as between nations) are getting worse, and the connection between societal collapse and these kinds of disparities is well documented. In short: things are a mess.

Underlying all of these crises is a cultural reality that makes them all the more frightening: from police violence to domestic violence to self-harm to international wars, we seem to default to violence over and over again as a problem solving tool. I think there are better tools available to us.

This moment is one of unprecedented changes and challenges that require more human ingenuity and cooperation than ever before. We are also in a time where learning to cooperate, learning to resolve things peaceably and make decisions grounded in our collective interests is rarely on the standard educational menu. Those who raise the possibility of such things are often treated like we are naive or escapist.

There is a permaculture principle that says that the problem is the solution. Is it possible that the large populations of marginalized, economically disenfranchised people with our eyes open to ecological crises (currently being labeled "a problem" by various people in power) might be able to come together collectively, and be the solution? I think so. This book is written in a spirit of solidarity with both the planet and the many marginalized peoples of the world in deep suffering. I am part of those masses; I am one of the many people simultaneously affected by what does not work in this world and working actively to change it.

I am writing for the people who want **collective** answers, and who see the deep benefits of community living as a key piece of that. I see community as a place to get the social connection we need to stave off what has been called a loneliness crisis, to share resources and lower our carbon footprints, and to have access to each other's creativity and let it spark our own so that when the crises hit close to home, we have the best possible chance of surviving them and even thriving in a new world.

I also take inspiration from many other movements and know that they are not separate from the communities movement. What many people picture when they think about community is oddly monoculture: we mostly think of young white people heading for rural places to start their version of utopia, or middle class people using the tool of community to create an even more comfortable and "safe" neighborhood for themselves.[2] Increasingly, the mainstream press is also profiling professional white people

---

2 Unfortunately, "safe" all too often implies surrounding ourselves with people who look, act, and communicate like me, and is one of the buzzwords that can make communities decidedly *unsafe* for many poor and working class, queer, gender-queer, and BIPOC (Black, Indigenous, People of Color) folks.

embracing co-living in urban areas. But those versions are far from the whole history (or current reality) of this movement.

Fannie Lou Hamer was a civil rights activist who rubbed shoulders with more well known Black leaders like Ella Baker and Malcom X, and lived communally for years in Wisconsin. The Black communal movement includes many notable figures and communities, including Hamer, MOVE in Philadelphia (still the only place to be bombed by the US government on US soil), and the community building activities in Jackson MS, organized under the umbrella of Cooperation Jackson.

Community has been used as an effective tool for economic sovereignty and liberatory political organizing for as long as community has existed. And of course the oldest human habitations on this continent were Indigenous Peoples with cultures more cooperative and oriented toward obligations to society rather than personal rights. The recent burst of indigenous-led and -centering intentional community projects is one of my brightest spots of hope right now. People who are more focused on their obligations to the people around them and the planet rather than their own individualistic rights are creating pockets of social and ecological resilience all over the world.

The urge for community to meet core economic needs is another thread worth tracing, and we don't have to go back very far at all for this one. When Covid 19 hit in 2020, people in the US experienced empty grocery shelves for the first time in many of our lives. Seed sales in 2020 skyrocketed, interest in all things "back to the land" jumped,[3] and mutual aid became a phrase no longer relegated to the fringes of socialist organizing and urban BIPOC (Black, Indigenous, People of Color) communities, springing into common usage seemingly overnight. Helping each other, and often doing it on the land in relation to our food and soil was the first thing many people reached for, and we saw this across the political spectrum.

While that sense of urgency has faded for many, the core truth of that moment remains. A return to deep, authentic relationship to each other and the land is part of what we all need to survive and potentially thrive when crises hit.

Several years before I decided to write this book, I was one of a handful of people involved in visioning a project for the Foundation for Intentional Community. We called it the Community Land Trust for Collective Liberation. The project description started with these two paragraphs:

> The Community Land Trust for Collective Liberation is being created to provide access to land for community projects that could not otherwise afford land. The

---

3   For one example, see: https://modernfarmer.com/2020/07/back-to-the-land/.

CLT will navigate the current legal and economic system to permanently remove land from the speculative real estate market and place its stewardship into the hands of people practicing justice and sustainability. Our work embodies the spirit of decolonization and reparations, and recognizes the primacy of land access for resilience, sustainability and stability for all peoples.

The CLT is a place of radical solidarity between poor and working class people, Black, Indigenous and people of color, and the land. The project uses the frameworks of intentional community and community land trusts, and is part of larger, growing movements for cooperative culture, collective liberation, and racial, economic and climate justice. Our Advisory Board and staff are made up primarily of people on the front lines of economic and racial justice struggles, and it is their understanding of practical needs and justice that drives our organizational priorities.

While this project has yet to get off the ground,[4] the vision is one that still encapsulates much of what motivates my work. I offer this book to the world in the spirit of the CLTCL: I believe that intentional communities with awareness of the social, economic, and ecological realities of our time are essential for the survival of humanity on the planet. Community is no longer an "interest area"; it is a necessity.

This book is written in part for those people who share my sense of urgency for the communities movement to be a significant player in shaping the next chapter of humanity, one that is in a deep and abiding relationship to land and with marginalized people. You can, of course, use this book even if your motivations are not identical to mine, and I hope all projects that use this book will be better for it. But you should be aware that I am going to frame many aspects in this book in terms of liberation and relational organizing, and hope you will join me in this orientation before you are through.

Just as there are many systemic reasons why the time is now to create community and return to cooperative stewardship of land, I am also tracking the personal, psychological, and often spiritual motivations for living in place-based community. Many of us realize that we cannot grow and mature into a greater experience of wholeness without becoming accountable to a circle of people and a place on earth. Community and land are both whole and complex systems that require deep personal reflection and responsibility to be in relationship with.

When we stay in a place, and deepen our emotional intimacy with people, we change. Often, we become more self aware, mature, wise, and able to see our impacts on

---

4   That said, we now have a BIPOC Council that has picked up some pieces of this work, and evolved their own direction beyond the original concept.

others and the world — both the good impacts and the bad. We learn to listen more deeply and speak with more intentionality. The learning journey of living in intentional community brings us in contact with our values and ethics, and we get to see where we have work to do.

While this is challenging to the ego, it ties us to the greater work of our times. Growing through whatever narcissistic tendencies and unexamined biases we've been trained into is **world** work, **culture change** work. It develops much needed personal skills for transforming systemic injustices.

An Interconnected World and a Colonial World

We do indeed live in an increasingly interconnected world: spiritually, economically, and socially. We literally evolved from mud and electrical charges in an ecologically interconnected world, and one way to measure the health of an ecosystem is by how many relationships are operating within it. But despite the fundamentally interconnected nature of things, there are very few places in the world not also sporting legacies of being built on stolen land and with enslaved labor — both of which are representative of a whole series of profound disconnections, and are rife with the complexities of privilege and trauma. How can we create movements and communities that appropriately reckon with this?

I'm attempting with this book to interweave answers to that question with a more nuts and bolts guidebook.

I know that many people who pick up this book just want me to tell you how to start a community. Sounds simple, right? A few checklists, some timelines, a little guidance on finding your land and a group, and voila! Community! Twenty or even ten years ago, I might have been able to write that book. Five years ago, I did include a chapter in *Together Resilient* which largely offered that kind of guidance. But even then, that chapter was in a book about the climate crisis. That crisis is one of the many reasons this book is no longer able to be that simple.

Cassandra Ferrera (who was an early consultant for this book) often talks about the lens of becoming a good ancestor. This is a book that tries to speak to that. Our friend Ridhi D'Cruz talks about the DNA of movements and how much they are in need of changing to get to a world of justice and sustainability. I am trying to speak to that as well. I intend to contribute ways of creating community that are not unquestioningly built on top of white supremacy and a profound disconnection from the earth.

Many of us who have been in this movement for a long time believe that meeting each other in circle (in community, with authenticity, humility, and courage) is part of how we become good ancestors and change the DNA of this movement. We also increasingly believe in not just meeting *on* the land, but meeting *with* it. Land is not just a surface to build buildings on and to landscape to be pleasing to the human eye. Meeting with the land is a process of listening, asking, and responding. It is the basis for liberatory relationships between humans and the planet we call home.

This is what I believe residential community creation can be: a liberatory space for genuine mutual aid between humans, and restored integrity between us and the lands we collectively steward.

This book interweaves the how-tos (the practical advice, and yes, plenty of bullet-pointed lists of things to do and consider) with the motivations and actions that can make this movement transformative for all beings on this planet. I write both as a 25+ year veteran of this movement and an experienced founder, as well as a woman dedicated to dismantling oppressive structures within a movement I love.

The slice of the movement I am most interested in supporting with this book is challenging social norms of privacy, isolation, and building security in a very personal, "look-out-for-number-one" way. Intentional communities often have collective values that challenge the basic assumptions of capitalism (whether they articulate it as such or not) and seek to share resources, reduce waste, and resolve conflict in ways that they hope will help repair the broken social and ecological world that they are differentiating from.

Anti-oppression work is not specific to the communities movement, but it is our work as much as every other movement's work at this time. Ultimately, I believe all true movements for justice and liberation are one movement: this thing we call the communities movement has the potential to be a land-based branch of that bigger movement in the same way that the Black farming movements and Land Back movements are. To live up to this potential, we will need to do this deliberately.

How I Came to This Work

To be totally honest, I was dragged kicking and screaming into my first community. I was pregnant with my son and their dad basically said, "I've been wanting to live in community ever since I spent a year on a Kibbutz in high school . . . now that we are having a kid, I feel like it's now or never." My response was not very charitable: "There's no frickin' way I'm moving to some stupid hippie commune in the middle of nowhere!"

My response was based on all kinds of stereotypes about communities: that they were escapist, drug-laden sex pits, and certainly no place to raise a kid. And I was wrong. Deeply wrong. I often say that I was stubborn but not stupid. It did not take long for me to look around at the community we had landed in and understand that here were people actually *doing* the things I had been *talking about* — intellectually exploring — for years as an activist, including feminism and sustainability work.

In many ways, community became my activism. I raised my son in a series of communities and still believe it is one of the best contributions I will ever make to the world. And I slowly learned how to become much more deliberate about my life choices: no longer getting dragged anywhere, I started to be able to create.

It was a mess a lot of the time. I was a mess a lot of the time. But I also learned. I particularly noticed a pattern: organization after organization (including community after community) failed in large part because people did not know how to cooperate, how to make decisions together, how to resolve conflicts. For many years, my community work focused on social dynamics.

In 2002, I got involved with the Foundation for Intentional Community because I saw deep value in the movement. I had seen enough by then to know that the struggles and failures I was seeing in my home communities were actually happening (with variations on the theme) all over the place, whenever people were attempting cooperation and communal living.

Over those years, I was in the role of founder four times. One I would call a resounding failure. Two were limited successes. The fourth made a huge difference in the lives of both the people who have lived there and the local community it influenced over the 5 years it was up and running.[5]

You learn stuff when it goes well. In some ways, you learn even more when it flops. What I bring into this book is both kinds of experiences. I've also now been teaching workshops and longer courses on starting a community for long enough that I've gotten feedback from people who took my advice (or didn't) and know a lot more about what actually works for more than just the groups I have had direct involvement with. The words you are reading come with a big load of gratitude to all of my co-founders, clients, and students over the years who have helped me refine this work, as well as the many

---

[5]   One of my most prized friendships from this community journey is with Dr. Zach Rubin, a researcher who focuses on community living. Zach has helped me shape my thinking on what "success" means and we both take a more activist and culture change approach to it these days. I consider Solidarity Collective to be a successful community start-up because of its impact, and I'm less interested these days in whether a community lasts for decades than I am in how it has helped change the world and lives in a positive way.

other founders I've been lucky enough to have deep conversations with about their own struggles and wins.

As you begin your own founder's journey, I'm happy to be in this with you and grateful for the opportunity to pass on a whole lot of people's wisdom in the form of this book.

The Invitation

Starting a community is hard work and intense personal growth, regardless of your intentions. I know I am asking you to bite off what can seem like "additional" pieces that will make this even harder in the name of creating a more just and equitable world through our community-making efforts. I do this because after years of observing this movement, and tracking global trends, I've come to believe that this particular version of "harder" is needed in order to build communities with the deepest possible lasting value to the world. I am asking this not just for you and your community mates, but also for the many people who would otherwise not be able to see themselves in your community, and, ultimately, for the next seven generations. I invite you to dream just that much bigger, and to see yourself as part of something deeply transformational, not just for you, but for all of us.

Sounds heavy and huge, right? It can be. I get it. But here's some of what makes it easier.

First, you are not alone. The deep longing for more authentic and real lives — together — is a bug that bites a large number of folks every year. For each one of you daydreaming about communal living, there are thousands of other people dreaming similar dreams. As you step into being a founder, know that you really are part of a much larger — and quite old — movement.

The dream to create a more whole and connected life is one that awakens in people of all walks of life, with various histories and levels of access to land and wealth. The yearning to belong to a place and a people could be said to be inherent in our very nature.

Second, the skills needed to create meaningful community are very similar to the skills needed to unpack oppression dynamics, and doing both sets of that work has great potential to be mutually reinforcing. You need to understand who you are, what role(s) you play in this life, how power works, and how resources are best used and directed for everyone's benefit, not just your own. Communities that are not a container for a dance between self-awareness and community good are not very strong communities, by any reasonable measure.[6]

Third, you have companions on this journey, including me. Many of us are active in sharing the things we have learned on that journey, and there is nothing theoretical here in this book. You do not have to figure it all out because many prior founders have stumbled our way through a lot of common mistakes, and we now know a heck of a lot about what not to do, as well as what to do.

My two prior books are additional resources for this work. *Together Resilient: Building Community in the Age of Climate Disruption* (2017) has chapters on legal and economic reform, and the cultural and emotional work, as well as profiles of a number of communities and projects that all have documented reduced carbon and ecological footprints. It is an especially good companion book for groups who are motivated by ecological resilience and sustainability, and would benefit from some community role models.

The Cooperative Culture Handbook: A Social Change Manual to Dismantle Toxic Culture and Build Connection (co-authored with Karen Gimnig, 2020) breaks down the many cultural and social dynamics that will create barriers to real cooperative work if left unexamined. It has 52 exercises in it that your facilitators and other leaders can use to help ease this transition and get to a place of functional community. Karen and I have articulated a kind of North Star to help guide the culture change aspects of community building and living. If you are as baffled and frustrated by your fellow humans as we often are, the *Handbook* will help.

The Journey in this Book

This book is divided into three sections: Setting the Stage, Defining and Materializing Your Community, and Transitioning to Community Life. Here's a very quick peek at each:

Part 1: Setting the Stage offers some context for this work: why (and why not) to start a community, traits of both good founders and good founding groups, a rough overview of phases that community start-ups typically go through, and an overview of types of communities. All of this is offered to help get you situated in this process.

Part 2: Defining and Materializing Your Community is the guts of the book and where almost all of the "how-to" stuff lives. I walk you through visioning, navigating culture

---

6   I'm going to stand by that statement, even though I can certainly think of examples of existing communities that embody a profound lack of self-awareness and have been around for decades.

and diversity, a brief[7] introduction to power, conflict and decision-making, membership and recruitment process recommendations, guidelines for developing money and labor systems, legal structures, property search, and finally some brief[8] guidance on basic community design.

Finally, Part 3: Transitioning to Community Life gives some advice and perspective for navigating the gap between being a founder and becoming a good community member.

Welcome to the journey!

---

7   Brief in this case because *The Cooperative Culture Handbook* is a whole book of my and Karen Gimnig's thoughts on this topic and there's no point repeating it all here.

8   Brief in this case because I absolutely should not write a book about design — this is not my zone of expertise!

CHAPTER 1:
MOTIVATION AND EGO MANAGEMENT

One of the universals of community start-ups is that someone or someones want something different from what mainstream society is providing. We have a vision of a better world and better lives. And while "better" means a lot of different things, it commonly includes some combination of more security, creativity, inspiration, ecological sustainability, equity, and connection. No one who is satisfied with the options "normal" life is handing us puts in the kind of work needed to create a community.

That said, there are a whole lot of reasons why you maybe shouldn't start a community.

Should you do this?

One of my obligations as someone who has been down this founder's road before is to make sure people enter into the project of founding a community with their eyes as open as possible. Ironically, I start my workshops by trying to talk people out of starting a community.[9] Consider the following as part of your decision-making process for starting a community.

It's a hard, long, and not simple journey.

Expect that it will be between two and seven years before you actually make it onto properly with your group. During that time, you will have to learn new skills, stretch out of your comfort zones (whatever they are), and deal with conflicts, tensions, and serious values questions with your group. You will spend many hours in meetings, watch people you come to care about come and go, do some of the most complicated planning work possible (and then throw half of it out the window six months later), and make hard compromises. Persistence, patience, and hard personal work are in your future if you decide to do this.

Have you considered getting a dog and starting a nonprofit or social benefit business?

While these questions are a little tongue in cheek, they have a serious underpinning to them. Most of us start a community because we have a sense of mission driving us: we

---

9   I've been told that this section in my workshops is one of the more memorable parts. Sometimes people even take it seriously. I've even had a couple people thank me a decade later for successfully talking them out of.

want a version of "something different." Sometimes, a residential piece isn't necessary to do that. It's worth at least exploring if there is a simpler option to effect the change in the world you want. Also: dogs are less complicated companions than humans. The point is, there may be simpler, easier, and less labor- and money-intensive ways to get your social needs met than a community of your own making!

Does something close already exist? Why not join?

There are thousands of already existing communities in the world, projects where a group of folks has already successfully navigated this complexity to get a project off the ground. Many of them need more people. If there is something similar to what you want, why not join one of these existing projects?

An underlying component to this question is that I guarantee the community you get *will not* ultimately be the one you're picturing now. Life will change what you want as you go through this process, other people will have visions as well and you will want to work with them to get as much of what you *all* want as possible, and sometimes reality intervenes with limitations you can't overcome. It is highly likely that what you get will be close but not exactly it . . . which means you might be just as well off joining something close and saving yourself years of labor and challenge.

What motivates you? How much of it is ego?

This is critical. It is so important, in fact, that I include this slide in my online workshops just to reinforce it:

There is definitely such a thing as a healthy ego: having strong enough self-esteem that you can navigate challenges without always coming away bruised and shaken. This is GOOD. However, you want to be very careful with this. If your motivation for starting a community is that you like the sound of "founder" next to your name, or you believe yours is the one true vision that will save the world . . . that's not a healthy ego.

You need some motivation for starting a community that transcends your own ego and is about selfless service to others and the planet. You have to genuinely want other people to show up and make your vision better. If you don't have this, the whole process is going to be unnecessarily complicated, you won't be much fun to live with, and you are unlikely to attract enough other healthy egos to do well.

I know people who have been "starting a community" for decades. Most of them don't lack commitment, passion, or reasonably good ideas: they lack ego management.

Imagine for a moment that starting a community is like painting a target on yourself: when things don't go well (which will inevitably happen some of the time) you, as the founder, will be the first person people look to if they are in a blaming mood. Ego-driven people tend to either fight back or crumple in that moment, neither of which goes well. You need to have something to reach for in that moment that pulls you out of yourself and lets you hear the feedback without defensiveness. If you don't have that, then don't do this.

Have you done your research? Toured existing communities? Talked to other founders? Read *Communities* magazine?

There is a wealth of knowledge out there already about how to do this well. An informed founder is much more likely to be a successful founder. The old saying holds here: learn from our pain. Have some conversations with other founders about what was hard, what they wished they had known before starting, etc. Take a course on starting a community. Find a mentor from a successful community to bounce things off of.

Communities magazine also contains decades of experience that you can easily access. I especially recommend the post-2016 years of the magazine (which is after the last publisher, FIC, started getting more serious about the inclusion of social justice in all of their publications, and generally the magazine took on a more authentic tone about the challenges and imperfections of this movement).

Finally, if you have the time and money to do a communities tour, I strongly recommend that. I'm always a little weirded out that people show up at my workshops on fire to start a community . . . but they have never actually visited one! If community living is still that theoretical to you, you are going to have a lot more trial and error in your future. That said, I recognize that not everyone is able to do this. Having the time, money and (in some cases) connections to make a good tour happen are all examples of privilege. For potential founders with disabilities and/or children, it can be even harder to do. So do it if you can, and if you can't, these other recommendations are also very helpful.

I particularly recommend visiting both communities that sound similar to what you want to create *and* communities that have some real differences. That may sound like weird advice, but here's what it is based on. When I first moved into community, I had an image of myself as someone who would just love to live in a cabin in the woods somewhere, pretty isolated and surrounded by the glories of nature. In this community I got the chance to do just that. It was great!

For about a month.

And then I started noticing these strange longings to be right in the middle of things. I found myself very drawn to living in one of the dorms instead of that sweet little cabin, and resenting the 10 minute walk to home. A few months later, my partner and I did a room swap and I was much happier — and slightly wiser — after that. Had I not had this experience, though, and had decided to start a community, I probably would have fought hard to get one where everyone had their cabin in the woods . . . only to come to hate my own creation.

So yes: please give existing communities a chance to teach you something new about yourself before you start the founding process.

Have you gathered other co-founders who balance out your weak points?

No one is good at the whole package of what it takes to get a community off the ground. Early on, you should be doing some good self-assessment and then looking for people who can balance you out and cover the other needed skills and traits (see the next section for the kinds of traits and skills I mean). Bring people close in to the process at the very early stages who think differently than you do and have different skills than you do because that kind of diversity is a strength. If you aren't able to do that, you won't get very far.

Maybe You *Should* Start a Community If . . .

The above list has a parallel list of good reasons to become a founder.

You crave a hard, long, and not simple journey.

Some of us hear "long, hard, not simple" and have an immediate "bring it!" response. Some of us get bored easily, and starting a community is an excellent antidote for boredom. If this is you, you could be a good founder.

The residential element *is* key to your vision.

If, after some contemplation, you come to the conclusion that the residential piece of your vision is actually essential (or is even the main point), then starting a nonprofit or social enterprise business won't be enough and you should probably proceed. (You can still get that dog, though . . .)

There isn't something close to your vision already, and you genuinely believe the world will benefit from it.

If you have something unique you want to pursue, then you should do it. (Notice there is a nuanced distinction between "my vision will benefit the world" and "my vision is what will save the world.") Communities are like little laboratories for social innovation and experimentation, and there are many benefits to people trying new things and being those innovators (especially if they see themselves as being part of a movement and share those stories to benefit others). Genuine uniqueness counts as a solid reason to start rather than join a community.

The world is in desperate need of real alternatives.

Again, I don't think narcissistic ego gratification is a good reason to do this, but people with healthy egos doing something that the world needs is an excellent one. And the world needs so many things right now: climate disruption resilient communities and low carbon consumption lifestyle demonstration projects; groups with deep commitments to racial justice and real economic security; the fostering of true mental health systems and cooperative schooling and childrearing; spaces where people with disabilities are not seen as an afterthought to be worked around but as humans deserving full access to life and influence; the preservation and expansion of core life skills like farming and home building.

These are just a few of the things that are desperately needed and intentional communities are uniquely suited to being those research and development spaces. If these are the kinds of things that motivate you, please do create a community!

You have a founder's urge strong enough that it can carry you through.

Some of us just seem wired to be starters. We are the ones in staff meetings suggesting more new projects than our workmates can handle, the ones who always bring up the big picture when everyone else just wants to plan a party, the ones up in the middle of the night, our brains racing three steps ahead. We may drive everyone else to distraction, but when combined with some solid follow through, we actually can create miracles. I've heard a few founders comment over the years that it was a relief to finally have a big enough project on their plate that they could finally focus on just one thing;[10] community can be an excellent channel for this kind of personality!

You are good at collaboration, sharing power *and* checking your ego.

This is a tough one, and it is on the "essentials" list. A lot of people check off all of the boxes up until now. It is rare to have both strong founder's urges and the ability to do it well *with other people.* But you are wanting to start something collective, not write the best monologue ever.

Spend some time really contemplating this one and ask some people who are close to you for their honest assessment of you as a leader and collaborator. Do you play well with others, even when someone else suggests the game? Can you take feedback well and grow into the person who is needed? Are you able to shift your perspective when you get new information or learn about the potential negative impacts on others of your ideas?

You are tied to a physical location and really want or need community.

Finally, even if not everything above is perfect, it may be that you just need to do this anyway. You might not be able to move somewhere that has existing communities. Maybe you are partnered with someone with kids and they can't leave the state, or have aging parents who need you close, or you love your kid's school and have another ten years before you'd feel good about leaving, or your job is just too good to leave. Community is a real need for many of us, and if there isn't anything already in our area, we find ourselves growing into being a founder because it is needed.

The upside to this last one is that connection to place is *also* a human need. Creating a community where you are instead of chasing the temptation of a perfect place elsewhere can be a powerful grounding for a new community project. If this is your scenario, I encourage you to lean into staying put as a strength. You have the gift of entering into partnership with place as a starting place. So what does this place need? You get to be part of that answer.

---

10 Albeit it a very large one thing.

Exercise 1: Motivation

Spend some time really considering why you are forming a new community. If it helps you to be more honest about it, just do this for yourself without any intention to share with others. You can use the above sections to help your contemplations. Here it is as a list of slightly reframed questions:

- Is there an easier way to get your social or mission-fulfillment needs met?
- Does something close already exist that you can join?
- What motivates you and how much of it is ego?
- Have you done your research?
- Have you gathered other co-founders who balance out your weak points?
- Are you ready for a hard and long journey?
- Do you play well with others?
- Is there really nothing close to your vision already that you could join?
- Do you genuinely believe the world will benefit from it?
- Do you have a founder's urge that's strong enough to carry you through?
- Are you tied to a physical location and really want or need community?

CHAPTER 2: WHAT MAKES A GOOD FOUNDER AND FOUNDING GROUP?

OK, so you are still with me, having decided that becoming a founder is really for you. Great! Now let's look at who you will need to become.

Some Traits and Skills of Successful Founders

I place a lot of emphasis on who you are and who you will become as someone taking on the founder's journey. Being a founder will challenge and change you. I offer here a list of traits and skills that you should consciously cultivate, either in yourself or your co-founders. And co-founders are essential.

Here is a (very partial) list as a starting place and to give you a sense of the breadth of what I mean.

- Fearless about realities
- Empathetic and listens well
- Good communicator (which includes verbal, written, and body language communication)
- Inspiring
- Humble and can set aside ego
- "Do whatever it takes" vibe
- Likes people (at least most of the time)
- Has a head for numbers
- Persistence and patience
- In touch with their own values and self-aware
- Flexible, can grow and change
- Kindness and generosity
- Resilience
- Even tempered
- Risk assessor . . . and risk taker
- Well organized
- Comfortable with conflict
- Savvy with oppression dynamics
- Lifelong learner orientation
- Research skills

One of the first ego lessons is recognizing that no one is good at all of these things (thank goodness you are doing something collective and other people can fill in for your weak spots!). Being "good" at these things is also a culturally loaded concept, and people who are neurodivergent can particularly feel like this list will never describe them. There are also some inherent tensions between some things on this list. For instance, it is rare to find someone who is both humble and embodies a "do whatever it takes" attitude, and risk takers may not always be paragons of patience. All of this adds up to you needing a team from the early days.

Skills and knowledge base of a founding group

Similarly, here are some of the skills and knowledge base a founding group should have (or be able to access).

Big Picture Skills:

- Organizational skills of all kinds
- Visioning, and ability to articulate the deepest version of that vision on the fly
- Planning and project management
- Big picture thinking
- Inspiring writing and speaking
- Tracking of details
- Understanding how your project fits (or doesn't) within various movements and trends

Social Skills:

- Networking
- Team and trust building
- Facilitation using cooperative methods[11]
- Governance experience with whatever system your group plans to use
- Able to engage with conflict productively and compassionately
- Mentoring
- Excellent listening and reflecting skills

---

11   To be clear, this does not include Robert's Rules. I encourage you to google it if you want to argue this point, but here's a couple data points. From Wikipedia on the origins: "A U.S. Army officer, Henry Martyn Robert (1837–1923), saw a need for a standard of parliamentary procedure while living in San Francisco. He found San Francisco in the mid-to-late 19th century to be a chaotic place where meetings of any kind tended to be tumultuous, *with little consistency of procedure and with people of many nationalities and traditions thrown together*." (My emphasis added). In other words, it was designed to shut down diverse ways of expressing ourselves and to keep the masses in check. See also this aptly titled article "Robert's Rules Suck": https://aninjusticemag.com/roberts-rules-suck-47b689f3c48f.

Economic Skills:

- Willing and able to source financing
- Spreadsheets and budgeting
- Financial management
- Business planning
- Legal savvy
- Understanding of systems of money, finance, and labor (and their impacts on relationships)
- Can connect systems decisions to daily quality of life and values

Physical Skills:12

- Construction, maintenance, and repair work
- Agriculture and/or landscaping
- Real estate development
- Land use planning
- Physical design (architecture, landscape, etc)

Contemplation exercise 2: Self-Assessment of Founder Traits

Take 30 minutes to contemplate and write in response to these two prompts:

1. What are your strengths and weaknesses as a founder?

2. Identify two or three things that you think are the most important to have someone besides you do.

About the founding group

What else do you need to know about gathering your initial core group? The above lists hint at something that is really important to keep in mind. Starting a community is not like other activist projects, nor is it simply about being a good neighbor. Starting a community is a little like starting a nonprofit (because of the deep mission and passion work), starting a small business (because of the need for business and legal savvy),

---

12 Especially during the development phase, some or all of these physical needs may be hired out for some communities. However, paying others to do all of this work can get expensive, so at a minimum, maintenance of spaces and landscape is usually held by the group themselves. And having someone in your group with the minimal skill of understanding what goes into the physical aspects of a development is invaluable.

getting married (because of the intense relational work involved), and doing a really intense and long term personal growth course (because, well, it is one).

All at the same time. With the same group of people.

Most of us have folks in our lives we might trust to start a business with, but are they the same people we trust to do intense and vulnerable relational and personal growth work with? And are those people the same ones with whom we share deep passions and an analysis of what the world needs? And do they want to live in the same places you are interested in living?

Maybe you're starting to see why putting together a founding group can be a real challenge. As someone who has been through this journey multiple times, it helps me to remember that list when I get down on myself about the failures. This. Is. Hard.

Here are four keys to having the right core group, in addition to the skills and orientations listed above.

1. **Everyone recognizes this is a long term commitment.** Again, expect this process to take two to seven years from the time you first start meeting. You can create a lot of disappointment for yourselves by not planning adequate time in your lives to do this well. As you go through this book, use it to create a realistic timeline and allow it to expand and contract organically as you go along. In order for people to stick with the project, you will collectively need to do a lot of expectations management, and the timeline is one of the most important parts of that.

2. **You trust each other.** Trust takes time to build and assess. Part of why the timeline is longer than most of us would like is that the social aspects of creating a community are not instant processes. Some other things that are essential (like determining your property search criteria or conflict resolution system) might be able to be completed over a few months, but trust building takes a lot longer.

3. **You have solid alignment on the core questions**. Choose your initial partners carefully, which probably means choosing your partners slowly. However, that doesn't mean your four best friends should be your founding group *unless you are very much on the same page about vision, values, and preferences for things like location, size of community, etc.* Use the spectrums exercise on page 51 as a tool for solo contemplation and then conversations to see if the alignment is strong enough to be a founding group together.

4. **Everyone can give this significant time (2–10 hours/week).** I've seen groups that meet several times a week for years to get particularly complex projects off the ground. I also know groups who think they can do this with a monthly two hour

meeting and not a lot in between. The latter groups either take a very long time to make progress, or they skip a lot of steps and regret it later. Your group will likely be something in between those two, but you need some core people who are going to make this a major focus of their attention. During the founding stage, you need burning souls who have the time and skills to ground this thing. Remember: you are doing something that our current culture and economic systems don't make easy. Take that into account when you feel like this thing is taking a lot from you: it is, and that is needed.

5. **You are between three and eight people.** That may seem weirdly specific, but here's my thinking. With three people you are more than just a couple, which is important for the dynamics of people joining you. Three people is enough that you *might* be able to have the skills and traits covered pretty well, and three minds are a lot more likely to recognize problems and challenges coming your way than one person alone. Eight, on the other hand, is about the highest number that you can do good, deep, initial decision-making with. More than that and it starts getting a lot harder to come to real alignment. Too many cooks in the kitchen too early can build fault lines into your project. They may not be problematic immediately, but could be disastrous down the road.

What if your group is already too big?

Many folks reading this will already have more than eight people in conversation, and you might be feeling very awkward at the moment. You also might have a group with very different levels of commitment and ability to put in the work.

My recommended way to work with both of these scenarios is to create what I have come to call a concentric circles structure. The core group in this case is the smallest group and it maps onto what I've been referring to as your founder group. A second ring out are folks who have some energy for the project, contribute well when they do show up, but aren't in a place where you can rely on them to be consistently showing up for the work. Those in this participating group are very likely to become members. The third circle, which can be as big as you want it to be, are the folks who are basically your interest list. They might be excellent joiners once there is something tangible to join, watching what you all decide to do before getting serious about it. They may show up for social gatherings, but not much else.

The main reason to do this is that trying to make decisions with people in very different places in terms of their commitment and seriousness is very uphill. I've watched groups stagnate for months or even years because they don't have this kind of clarity.

I encourage you to spend time fleshing out a list of both rights and responsibilities for each circle, with the core group being stronger on both fronts. (See Figure 1 for a little more detail.) Then look at the list of folks who are currently involved and make an honest attempt to sort people into these three circles. Share the framework and the proposed sorting with the group. (Interestingly enough, sometimes people will ask to be considered in a different circle during this process, either realizing they don't have as much to give right now as they thought they did, or having the sorting itself spark a desire to commit more deeply. Unless you have serious trust issues with someone wanting to be closer in, it is probably pretty safe to let people land where they are comfortable with this.)

Finally, you will want a clear articulation about how someone moves toward the center. (People should be able to drop back voluntarily at any time without much fuss.) Once you are further into the process, you will want to have a more thorough and fleshed out membership process (see Chapter 8 for more on this) and the work you do now is good practice for that later process.

CONCENTRIC CIRCLE MODEL
TO SORT EARLY PARTICIPATION*: AN EXAMPLE

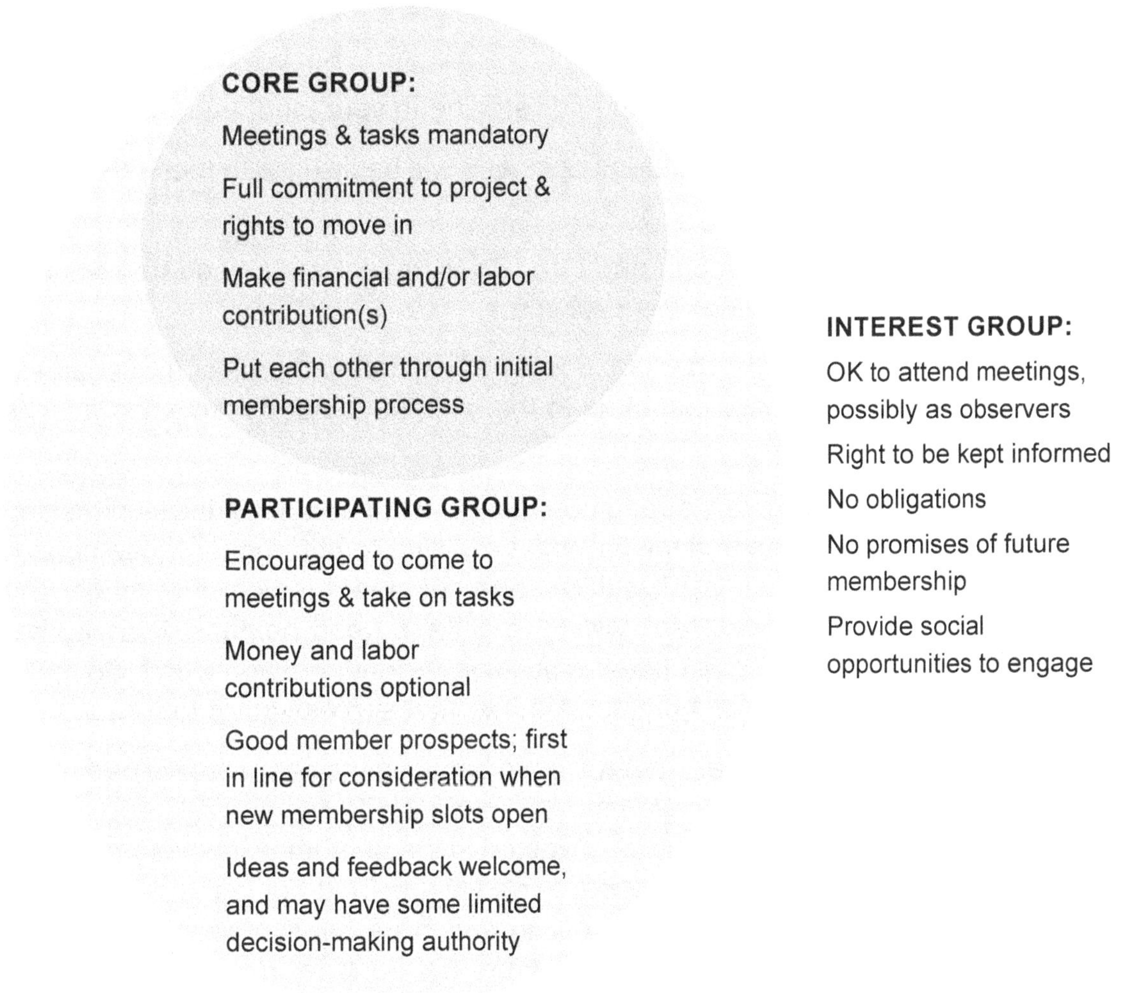

CORE GROUP:

Meetings & tasks mandatory

Full commitment to project & rights to move in

Make financial and/or labor contribution(s)

Put each other through initial membership process

PARTICIPATING GROUP:

Encouraged to come to meetings & take on tasks

Money and labor contributions optional

Good member prospects; first in line for consideration when new membership slots open

Ideas and feedback welcome, and may have some limited decision-making authority

INTEREST GROUP:

OK to attend meetings, possibly as observers

Right to be kept informed

No obligations

No promises of future membership

Provide social opportunities to engage

***Note that this sorting will cease to be used once the community is established and the regular membership process takes over**

Figure 1: The Concentric Circles Model

The challenges with "developer driven" community

When a project is developer driven, you have a partner who is in it for profit. They may also be in it for other things, but profit is introduced as a core decision-making criteria. Their need for profit will drive decision-making timelines and priorities in ways that may prevent the group from going at a pace that:

1. is thoughtful and deliberative,

2. allows for social bonding,

3. lets you work in real connection with and listening to your land, and

4. allows real input gathering from the people who will be living with these decisions for many years to come.

They may also want to make enough profit that it will undermine any goals you have around affordable housing and economic justice.

That said, you need the kind of expertise, access to capital, and project management skills that many good developers can bring to the table (if you don't have that access and skills in the group already).

I strongly recommend creating very strong boundaries and domains of decision-making if you have an outside developer involved, and be willing to both honor those boundaries and insist they do as well. Work with them to get clear together that profit can't trump vision and people. If they aren't willing to strike a good balance, find another partner. Most developers will leave once the building is done, but you won't. So make sure they are really going to do this project in a way that serves your priorities.

In those cases where the developer **doesn't** leave because they are actually part of the group, this clarity of roles becomes even more important, Playing that role and having to dance between being a group member, invested in the outcomes in a very personal way and having group member level concerns and wants, and being the driver of the building process at the same time is exhausting and stressful. I've seen some really good people do this dance, and most of the time their long term relationships with others in the group have been negatively affected by it.

If there is any way to avoid this, I strongly recommend it. If you have to do it for some reason, then please try to get very clear about how this person will know when they are in each role and help them sustain that clarity throughout the process. Make sure as well that they are compensated reasonably for their time as the developer and not expected to just be giving away lots of hours of highly skilled labor that they may not be able to afford to give away. (This one task alone is definitely over the 2–10 hours/week that I'm suggesting is to be expected of the founder group!)

Exercise 3: Getting the Right Core Group

If you already have a core group

- Spend the time thinking about what they bring and if there are any missing pieces.
- Think as well about how well you really fit together as a group.
- Are there questions you can think of to ask to better determine alignment? (The spectrums exercise on page 51 can help with this.)

If you do not yet have a group

- Spend the time making notes on what is going to be most important to balance you out.
- Are there specific people you would like to invite to join you? If possible, name names and how you will approach them.

CHAPTER 3: PHASES OF COMMUNITY CREATION

Different phases of community creation need different kinds of work, focus, and people. Here's a very rough and simplified sense of what those different phases will look like.

Phase 1: Set the core patterns for this community.

This is when you will determine the basic nature of this community. Your initial core group will ideally have those three to eight people we talked about in the last chapter (enough to get some diversity of skills and ways of approaching things, but not so many people that it will be hard to reach agreement on these big picture topics). While personalities will vary, everyone in this first group will likely have some entrepreneurial, starter energy and be comfortable with risk taking.

This phase also sets the pattern for how your community deals with conflict as the first tensions will almost certainly arise during this phase. I strongly recommend getting professional support for learning decision-making and conflict resolution skills during this phase, with the goal of creating a solid enough container for brave and compassionate authenticity as core social traits of your group. That said, be wary of the "all work and no play" dynamic — this phase can take a while to get through . . . make sure you are enjoying it!

Where to find pieces related to this phase in this book:

- Vision and values: Chapter 5
- Decision-making system: Chapter 7
- Membership processes: Chapter 8
- Economic structure: Chapter 9
- Labor structures: Chapter 9
- See also: *The Cooperative Culture Handbook*

Phase 2: Property acquisition.

You can now grow your group, and will probably have to. In this phase, you will create a business plan, fundraise, determine your property purchase criteria and create a legal structure. It's fine (and even good) to have some folks join you in this phase who are more of the joiner types and a bit more cautious, especially if they have good planning skills. If you get bigger than 8 at this point, that's OK.

You may have talked about some of this in the first phase, but this is the time when you get very concrete. Regardless of how you see yourselves being funded, the level of detail a bank would probably want to approve a loan is a realistic guide for how clear you need to get to reduce the likelihood of hard financial challenges down the road.

You want to build up your group size to the point that you have a few more people than you think you need for property purchase and the financial commitments of the first few years. Having more than enough is wise because property purchase is one of the predictable moments when most groups lose some people. (See the sidebar on page 35 for more of those common dropout moments.)

Early in this phase, you will be watching the real estate market in the area you want to end up, and thinking through practicalities like what kind of utilities are best aligned with your vision, how food-self-sufficient you want to be, etc. In short, this is the phase where you start shifting from a visionary and social group into one with much more attention on the physical and economic aspects of your project. This phase ends when you buy property (which may mean signing a deal with a member for the group to take over ownership of one of their properties).

Where to find pieces related to this phase in this book:

- Business planning: Chapter 9
- Legal structure: Chapter 10
- Property search criteria: Chapter 11
- Design basics: Chapter 12
- Pre-move in checklist: Chapter 13

Phase 3: Early days transitioning to living together, with two variations.

Phase 3a: The building it version. This is what needs to happen when you buy either raw property or a property with only some of the structures you will need for long term living. This phase may involve contracting with contractors and architects, a lot of group meetings to set design parameters and approve designs as your professionals bring them to you, and fleshing out your priorities as expressed in physical space. In other words things like how much to prioritize common facilities over personal ones, how much to build for full life cycle living, etc.

It is important during this phase to not lose focus on your social needs and vision. As you work your way through this phase, you may be needing to get new people on board to sell units or fill out labor needs prior to moving onto the property together. Orienting and mentoring new folks is just as important as finalizing building plans, but very easy to lose sight of with the urgency of building timelines.

(Note: you will also go through a lot of what I have in phase 3b, either in sequence or mixed in together, depending on whether you are building gradually or building out the community in one big push at the beginning.)

Where to find pieces related to this phase in this book:

- Conflict: Chapter 7
- Budgeting: Chapter 9
- Design Basics: Chapter 12

Phase 3b: The moving onto built out property version. You will probably continue growing the group in this phase. This tends to be a chaotic time when the realities of living together start to come home. Depending on the particulars of the property you chose, you may also need to figure out how a property that may not have been built for long-term communal purposes is going to work for you. There may be walls to move and spaces to repurpose, and there will almost certainly be significant time spent figuring out how to best manage and divvy up access to spaces.

There is both more excitement and more conflict in this phase, and that conflict can be of a more mundane nature, and might even feel relatively petty. You are working the kinks out of systems in this phase, and people who are good at identifying problems and solving them are especially valuable, as are people skilled in conflict resolution, particularly if they are bold enough to help the founders through the defensiveness that often arises as some of their theoretical thinking from that first phase turns out to not work so well in real time and space.

Phase three will typically last from 1 to 5 years. At the end of it, you will ideally be close to your target population size.[13] You will also officially transition from the founding journey and move into the established community journey.

Where to find pieces related to this phase in this book:

- Conflict: Chapter 7
- Becoming a good community member: Chapter 14

---

13 This won't, of course, be true if you have a vision of eventually being a small town as a few communities have done. Your phase 3 and 4 will likely be blended for a very long time.

Phase 4: Settling in for the long haul.

In phase 4, you will have worked out a lot of initial kinks, and you will have your major systems established and mostly tested out. This is the best phase to bring in people who need stability, and folks who are good at maintaining systems. Some of your founders may start getting bored and restless and some of them will move on once the energy shifts into this phase, while others may be carrying a sense of history that colors their interactions with newer folks. (See pages 200 - 203 on Founder's Syndrome for more about what I mean by this.)

At this point, a challenge is how to bring new people in with new ideas and energy and have them be well oriented, welcomed, and trained in systems, while keeping the door open for innovations and changes. This is the phase that most of us picture when we are starting a community: a fully realized vision with systems like gardens, buildings, working and eating together, etc. It is unlikely to perfectly match up the pictures we had in our heads at the beginning, but this is the phase when most of us are able to start looking around with some real satisfaction and enjoy the fruits of our significant labor.

It is not unusual for groups in the 12–20 year age range (from when the founders started) to find themselves needing a vision and values refresh, and that moment can be fraught for the founders who are still around. In some ways, this might be seen as a fifth phase: the community reboot.

Where to find pieces related to this phase in this book:

- Founder's syndrome: Chapter 14
- Review content from Chapters 5, 6, 7, and 8 and *The Cooperative Culture Handbook* as revisions become necessary, and to help you not stagnate as you mature

Predictable Drop Out Points in the Founding Journey

A lot of people are excited about community living, yet only a fraction of them ever end up in a project as a resident. There are a lot of reasons for this gap, but one of them is that, while the dreaming is fun, the reality of the hard work and need to compromise along the way isn't much fun. More significantly, sometimes the compromises needed are ones that someone can't make and still feel like the project is well enough aligned with their own values and needs.

Here are a few typical points in the process that cross the "shit just got real" line for different people, and you should expect (or not be surprised) to lose some folks:

- **The vision gets pinned down.** If you are doing alignment that goes deeper than a surface-level feel good and into something usable that will distinguish you from other projects, people who aren't fully aligned will often step away.
- **The first real conflict.** Interpersonal conflict scares the crap out of most people, and community living is a high stakes place to have tensions. This is a moment that, if handled well, can bring people closer in and build confidence. But most groups don't yet have the skills for this first round (or the first several) to be a positive experience, and some people will opt out.
- **Business planning.** Money is a really hard topic for a lot of people, and few people love business planning. And unless you prioritize financial accessibility, you will lose some people simply because they can't afford to join the kind of community you are creating.
- **Property purchase.** Most of us have pictures in our minds of what "our" community will look like, and the real property you end up choosing might not be a close enough fit for some. If people can't flex to adjust their mental pictures to match the reality, expect some folks to step out at this point.
- **Moving in.** This is another point where unaddressed misalignments can cause some folks to walk away. It is also the last doorway between dreaming and living, and for some people, this is ultimately more fun to dream about than to do.

I'm sharing this list so that you are less likely to be caught off guard when you lose folks you've been building relationships with for a while. Here's two real community examples of times that members were lost at one of these points.

Dancing Rabbit Ecovillage was once a small group of founders who moved from California to Missouri to start a community. The core group rented a trailer across the road from the property they had purchased and continued their intensive work of planning together. They'd always talked about having a relatively dense human settlement in one part of the property, but a couple of the founders, when faced with that reality, started to lobby the rest of the group to change to a homesteading model where each family unit would have more acreage to work with at the homestead level.

The founders describe this as an early really hard moment when they had to decide between sticking with the vision, or keeping everyone involved. They stuck with the plan and lost a few key people in the process. The benefit of that decision, however, was the creation of a unique and vibrant community model.

One of my own groups, Solidarity Collective, purchased a property with five founders. We had a business plan that worked well with 8–10 people, but a property showed up that was already built for more communal purposes and we decided to jump. Within a month of the property purchase, one of the couples came to the group with some pretty inflammatory statements about trans folks, and the rest of us asked them to step out since we placed a high value on being a safe space for the LGBTQIA+ community.

In both of these examples, the founders did what I consider to be the right thing and put the purpose of the community ahead of the individuals who figured out they wanted something different. That did put strain on both groups, but both projects were ultimately stronger for it.

CHAPTER 4: TYPES OF COMMUNITIES

This is a brief tour of this movement you are signing up to be a part of. This section is my version of laying out some categories of communities to hopefully help you feel at home in your communities world niche. If this isn't of interest to you, feel free to skip ahead. There is nothing in this chapter that you need to know for starting a community.

The next chapter is about visioning your community for the greatest likely success. I provide useful tools and perspectives to help you do a thorough, concrete, and thoughtful job with visioning. This chapter on types of communities is intended to help get some creative juices flowing for you, and also to provide a little context for your project in the larger scheme of things. You can also explore more about the current makeup of the movement through the Communities Directory, online at www.ic.org/directory or by getting a hard copy of the Directory.[14]

An Overview of the Communities Movement

There are a lot of different ways to categorize kinds of communities, and there's nothing magical or more right about how I do that than how others might frame it.[15] Still, it's useful for a lot of folks in their early stages of this journey to have a sense of the lay of the land of the movement. For me, what is most interesting is the *motivations* we have for starting and joining community, and so I map them on that basis. I'm also giving these to you in *roughly* historical order of their emergence.

My organizational structure yields eight categories:

1. Spiritual or Religious

2. Cultural Preservation

3. Social Experimentation

4. Service-based

5. Economic Security

6. Identity-based Safe Havens

7. Lifestyle and Comfort Enhancement

8. Ecological Sustainability

---

14 https://www.ic.org/community-bookstore/product/directory-book/.

15 Cynthia Tina and I did a fun self-paced course together in 2022 where she laid out a different way of organizing this. You can find it at: https://www.ic.org/intentional-community-basics/.

Here's a brief profile of each type:

The oldest intentional communities were probably **spiritual or religious** in nature, motivated by a desire for support for spiritual beliefs or practices, and mechanisms like the power of a collective to allow a vow of poverty to not be a vow of misery. If you believe in the historical versions of these religious leaders, you could say that Jesus and Buddha were kind of the great-great-great-etc.-grandfathers of the communities movement in that they both encouraged followers to band together into groups, de-emphasize possessions and wealth, and emphasize spiritual growth in a collective setting. Many modern versions of these exist: ashrams, nunneries, monasteries, abbeys, and a host of other types of religious and spiritual communities that do not neatly fit with those labels.

Some communities form around a motivation of **cultural preservation**. The wider culture is changing too fast and in a direction that doesn't match their values or meet their needs. I had a lot of Amish and Mennonite neighbors in my Missouri years, and I see their settlements and collective work and values preservation as another type of intentional community. The resistance to colonialism and organizing around language and traditional knowledge and spiritual practice that Indigenous Peoples engage in all over the world is another urge for collective cultural preservation, such as the Ekvn-Yefolecv Ecovillage Project.[16] You could also classify back to the land groups that reject the use of electricity and other modern technology as preservation communities. Despite their very different political and social beliefs and positioning, these groups are all serving the purpose of preserving and revitalizing traditional skills and knowledge.

On the other hand, some people feel like the culture isn't changing fast enough, and they launch a community for the purpose of (very broadly defined) **social experimentation**. These groups are pushing the envelope on something, including experiments in more authentic interpersonal relationships (like Ganas Community on Staten Island), new social or economic structures (like the many groups inspired by the book Walden II), and polyamory (including the much-studied historical Oneida community, and Kerista Community, one of the more influential polyamory projects in the US). This group also includes groups motivated by justice and anti-oppression work, where people create a space to live in new and different systemic relationships.

---

16 In the words of co-founder Marcus Briggs-Cloud, "The organization Ekvn-Yefolecv [*ee-gun yee-full-lee-juh, a double entendre meaning Returning to the Earth/Returning to Our Homelands]* is a Maskoke collective committed to embracing the role of protecting and reviving traditional relationships to the earth while revitalizing language and culture." Quoted from https://abladeofgrass.org/articles/a-radical-re-settlement/.

Service-based communities form a whole other subset of the movement. The roughly 190 Catholic Worker Houses[17] worldwide have long worked in solidarity with homeless populations. Zen Houses have similar intentions. Grounded in the work of Rudolph Steiner, the whole Camphill Communities movement has done some really interesting work re-envisioning a meaningful life for both people with developmental disabilities and those who love them.[18] Many communities have service at their heart, whether that means structuring the whole community around it, or simply running programs that serve the broader community in some way (everything from rites of passage and educational programs to providing space for local activists to meet to running a bulk food buying club that serves more people than just their members).

Economic security is a significant and growing motivation for creating community. The Rochdale Principles[19] originally came out of the labor movement in the UK, and offered the first formal articulation of what we now call cooperatives. These principles have been applied to everything from grocery stores to worker collectives to housing. Artists communities in many urban areas have preserved affordable rent in some of the worst housing markets in the country for many years using the cooperative model. The North American Students of Cooperation[20] (NASCO) supports coop houses all over the US, including large populations of communalists in Ann Arbor, Madison, and Austin. NASCO is a great resource for folks interested in exploring this model more.

The People of Color Sustainable Housing Network[21] in California's Bay Area was started to specifically counteract gentrification in one of the most expensive housing markets in the US. Similarly, income sharing communities (including communes, with the added feature of having egalitarian decision-making), where people pool their funds and are working toward egalitarian distribution of goods, are a particularly interesting tool in times of economic insecurity. (I'll say more about communes in Chapter 9 on economic structures.)

---

17 "Catholic Workers live a simple lifestyle in community, serve the poor, and resist war and social injustice. Most are grounded in the Gospel, prayer, and the Catholic faith, although some houses on this list state that they are interfaith. Each Catholic Worker house is independent and there is no 'Catholic Worker headquarters.'" Catholic Worker Houses have their own directory: https://www.catholicworker.org/communities/directory-picker.html.

18 https://www.camphill.org/ "Camphill is a worldwide social initiative that creates communities designed to include people with and without intellectual disabilities. We strive to empower people to grow, learn, and achieve together."

19 https://en.wikipedia.org/wiki/Rochdale_Principles.

20 Despite what the name implies, NASCO houses are not just limited to student housing.

21 https://www.pochousingnetwork.com/ "We are committed to creating an entire ecosystem of POC-centered co-housing, cooperative housing, and intentional communities that are ecologically, emotionally, spiritually and culturally regenerative spaces." I interviewed Noni Session and Greg Jackson of the POCSHN's East Bay Permanent Real Estate Cooperative on episode #3 of the Solidarity House podcast. It's a remarkable project. https://solidarityhouse.podbean.com/e/cowboys-on-the-commons-3-struggles-for-economic-justice-11918/

From war resistance to LGBTQIA+ enclaves to liberatory organizing for Black power, **identity-based safe havens** are another reason people do community. The oral history that was passed down to me in my early days working with the Foundation for Intentional Community[22] (this book's publisher) was that FIC had its roots in WWII war resistor communities that formed a network of mutual aid and communications. But in my lifetime, I haven't ever seen a "war resistor" community form. Based on that and seeing the growing number of LGBTQIA+ communities that *have* formed, I've come to the conclusion that there is an interesting correlation between the politics of the day in any given place and what kinds of communities form in that place and time.

Essentially, when a society is unsafe for a subset of people, community is a common response to the need for safety and companionship, and at times the lack of safety can even extend to active government suppression. It also (perhaps non-intuitively for some) allows people to be identified as more than their marginalized identity because that identity is *how they belong*, not *how they are set apart*. In other words, if you are gay in the wider world, lots of attention goes to being gay. If you are gay in a place where you are surrounded by mostly other gay people, you have a lot more energy to explore all the other parts of yourself, and you get to be more of a whole person.

In contrast to the urges for survival, **lifestyle comfort and enhancement** also motivate some groups to form. Having a safe and comfortable neighborhood in which to retire or raise your kids, not having to drive far to be with friends, and having access to more amenities for less or the same amount of money (such as a commercial kitchen and large dining room, a hot tub, guest rooms, land for walking and gardening, etc.) are examples of motivations that focus on enhancing individual comfort through a communal mechanism. In the US,[23] much of the Cohousing movement has ended up filling this niche, being a form of community that is the "live the good life" version of community. It's helped create significantly more acceptance in the wider culture (both the media and the banking industry) for the communities movement as a whole. The Cohousing Association of the United States[24] keeps a smaller directory up to date with just cohousing projects.

Finally, a growing number of communities are motivated by finding a way to embody **ecological sustainability**. The "ecovillage" label is a relatively new one, but the urge to

---

22 FIC can be found at www.ic.org. It is the publisher of this book among others, was the publisher of *Communities* magazine for many years, and is the home of both the *Communities Directory* and many online courses and other resources for the communities movement.

23 This is in contrast to the roots of Cohousing in Denmark where the ecovillage and cohousing movements are much more closely aligned than the US.

24 https://www.cohousing.org/. Their mission reads: "Spreading the word about cohousing shifts the culture toward a new American dream where every home is surrounded by caring, collaborative neighbors who use less of the earth's resources while living an abundant life."

live more simply has been with us for a long time. What the writings and communities of Arthur Morgan,[25] traditional wisdom in Indigenous villages all over the world, communes with demonstrated economic and ecological savings, and modern ecovillages all have in common is the sense of humans and land as a partnership more than a domination game.[26] With the rise of multiple ecological crises (climate disruption, species extinction, ecosystem collapses, etc.) this motivation is bringing a rising number of people to the communities movement. The Global Ecovillage Network[27] is an international organization active in nearly every region of the world supporting everything from forming ecovillages to groups that have been around for a half century or more.

These eight categories have fuzzy boundaries between them. For instance, is Twin Oaks, a Walden II inspired commune with one of the lowest ecological footprints of any studied settlement in the US in the social experimentation, economic security, or ecological sustainability categories? The answer is: all three. And that's just fine.

And would my Amish or Indigenous neighbors really want to be considered to be part of an intentional communities movement? Maybe or maybe not. My intention here is to document why people do community, to normalize these urges, and to help you see yourself as part of a vibrant and growing movement with a very rich and varied history, and not (as too often gets said) something people tried in the 60s and failed at.[28] My intention is not to impose an unwelcome label on any group, and groups should feel free to embrace seeing themselves as an intentional community or not.

---

25 https://en.wikipedia.org/wiki/Arthur_Ernest_Morgan.

26 I documented some of these savings for both communes and ecovillages in *Together Resilient: Building Community in the Age of Climate Disruption*, 2007, published by the Foundation for Intentional Community.

27 https://ecovillage.org/. "The Global Ecovillage Network envisions a world of empowered citizens and communities, designing and implementing pathways to a regenerative future, while building bridges of hope and international solidarity."

28 I could write a whole other book about all the things I dislike about that narrative. Laird Schaub tells a hilarious and frustrating story of being at a dinner gathering with an academic years ago and having his dinner companion insist that "all the counterculture communes failed miserably" and refusing to hear from Laird that he had literally started one of them in 1974 that was very much still alive. Fortunately, most academics have done better research than that guy. I encourage the curious to look into the work of the many scholars active in the Communal Studies Association (https://communalstudies.org/) and International Communal Studies Association (http://www.communa.org.il/icsa/index.php/en/) to learn more about the richness of this worldwide movement and its history.

PART 2: DEFINING AND MATERIALIZING YOUR COMMUNITY

CHAPTER 5: VISIONING YOUR COMMUNITY

Now that you have a sense of the territory you are going to be playing in, let's turn our attention to what *you* want to do.

Visioning

One of the most fun parts of starting a community is visioning. Ideally, your vision will be joyful and inspiring, but also actionable and effective at moving your project forward in a coherent way. I've found there to be four essential keys to a good visioning process for communities.

1) Know thyself. As one of the first people involved in this project, your level of self-awareness is going to set the tone for the community as a whole. The more clear-eyed you are about what you want and why, the better this will go for everyone. At this stage, clarity and clear communication are what will serve you best. That said, sometimes founders think they need to have answers to everything: you don't. You just need to be real about what is important to you.

To get clear about what you want in some of the core traits of communities, I recommend using the Spectrums for Intentional Communities exercise on page 51 to help determine where you are more attached, and where you don't have strong needs or opinions. That discernment is essential. Being flexible wherever you can leaves space open for other people's visions to be able to enhance yours, and so it is just important to get clear about where you don't have strong preferences. Be real about the answers you do have and the things that are essential to your vision — compromising on those things will just lead you to be unhappy, and will likely build in fault lines to the project as it gets more real and you have unmet needs. But when you find you don't have a particular opinion or need in some area, that's actually a gift to the other people in your group and it is healthy to let other people fill in those blanks.

2) Do it early, but not solo. Remember: YOU are not a group! This visioning work is often the first real chance to practice sharing power. A vision that deeply resonates with six people is much more likely to be attractive to more people than one that is just based on the passions and preferences of one person.

3) Balance! You must be specific enough so people know what they are joining, but not so prescriptive that others won't be able to see themselves in it. A common mistake among founders is thinking that it is better to "wait until the whole group is here" to determine your vision. This leads to a particular kind of messiness where you either 1) can't get agreement on anything meaningful because you waited too long and there are now too many cooks in the kitchen, 2) no one really commits because they can't see a clear vision of what they are committing to, or 3) the group splinters once the real differences emerge and you find yourself back to a smaller core group anyway. (See sidebar for a story about this phenomenon.)

Learning from my pain on visioning

I was a co-founder of a project from 2004-2007 that we called the Zialua Ecovillage (ZEV) and felt lucky to be working closely with two other women who I was very good friends with. The three of us formed the core of the group. We were all dynamic and committed. What we weren't was aligned.

One wanted a group that focused a lot on the intersection of spiritual work and sustainability and didn't have particularly strong opinions about structure. One wanted something quite communal and was drawn to properties such as a former monastery that came on the market while we were in development and already had infrastructure that emphasized sharing over personal space. She emphasized formal membership processes. The third was all about business development and liked an N Street Cohousing[29] model where people would buy up houses on the same block and take fences down to make more organic shared spaces but preserve personal ownership of homes. She didn't really care much about knowing who was formally "in" the group and who wasn't. We all loved gardening and used a lot of the same language to talk about what we were doing.

All three of us were active in recruiting people in. And there's where the problems started to emerge. Essentially, we each emphasized what we were picturing in our heads, and so we ended up with three pretty different groups of people who found themselves in meetings together that were confusing and frustrating. We hadn't taken the time to get well-aligned and to move past the "Rorschach words" stage of visioning. Eventually things melted down, and what finally ended up happening was the "low hanging fruit" vision of an interesting city block, with no formal membership designation. It wasn't a failure, but it never really became a coherent community either.

---

29 https://www.ic.org/directory/n-street-cohousing/.

Do enough work with your small core group to be able to make a clean invitation, but keep it open enough that people can live into it authentically for themselves. This can be a tricky balance to strike, but one you need to pull off. I've seen aspiring founders create 30-page documents with a prescriptive level of detail, and then wonder why no one wants to join them. What they don't seem to understand is that all it takes is a few key details that sound unappealing for most people to say no thank you and go looking for home somewhere else . . . and in a 30-page document, nearly everyone save the writer themselves will be able to find some reason to not engage.

The best inviting and clear vision statements are between a couple paragraphs and a couple pages in length.

4) Beware the Rorschach words. Rorschach blots are those black and white inkblots that aren't really anything. They are used by psychologists to help gain insight into someone's psychology by noting what someone "sees" in them. The value of them is that they could literally be anything and whatever people see is almost entirely a product of their own minds.

Community vision statements sometimes look like a collection of Rorschach blots that people can project damn near anything on. I call these words that are easy to project things on "Rorschach words." Some classic examples that appear in a huge percentage of communities' mission statements are: sustainable, affordable, community, respect, diversity, and safety.

Visions and values work are important for a few reasons. One is recruitment, and I've already mentioned some of the dynamics around that. Another is decision-making. Ideally your vision work provides a guide to keep the group on track in terms of their mission. Rorschach words are a disaster for both of these.

First, if anyone can project anything on most of the key words in your mission statement, then there is a very low level of actual alignment happening in the membership process. You may be a little more aligned than a general cross-section of the population, but it is a very ephemeral kind of alignment.

Second, for decision-making, things need to be specific enough to actually help when the rubber meets the road. Does "sustainable" mean you will have a recycling center and EV charging station in the parking lot? Or does it mean you are going to try to operate on 10% of the US average of carbon emissions?[30] Those are radically different practical applications, but both are reasonable interpretations of the word.

---

30 Yes, this can be done. See my 2013 TEDx talk, *"Sustainable is Possible!"* (under the name Ma'ikwe Ludwig).

Does "safety" mean you will accept me, even when I occasionally lose it and yell? Or does it mean people have the right to never be around raised voices? Safety can mean almost the exact opposite things to different people and you need to either be clear what the practices are that will express "safety" or pick another word that is less open to interpretation (and, frankly, less culturally and socio-economically laden).

The point is, you really need to define these words in concrete terms, and do it before you start inviting people in. Then you need to be prepared to talk about your unfolding understanding of what these things mean as a regular feature of your decision-making, conflict resolution, and culture-making processes.

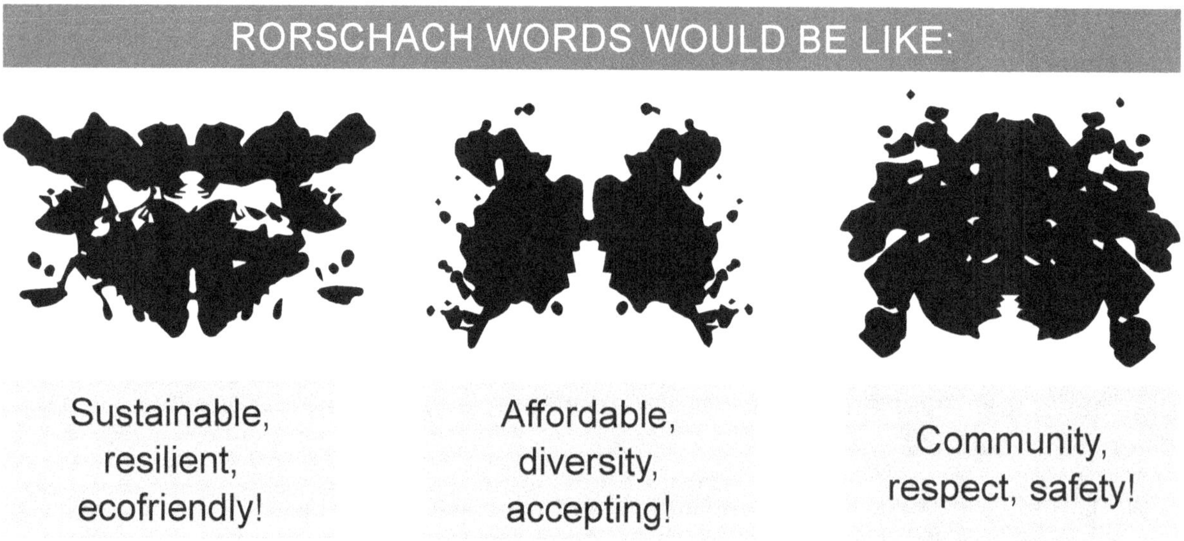

Figure 2: Beware the Rorschach Words

Spectrums for Community Visioning

One of the most valuable tools I've developed for forming communities is this set of spectrums. Essentially, every community falls somewhere on each of these spectrums, either deliberately or by default. Default is not necessarily bad: you being flexible about some of this and letting it emerge organically means that other people will have as much say in that piece as you do. This is a key tool for fulfilling both the "Know Thyself" and "Balance" criteria mentioned above.

I've already mentioned the common phenomenon of founders making the mistake of thinking that they can answer all these questions after they have a group of people they really like who have decided to join. The pitfall in waiting to get clear about that is that you run the risk of not having enough alignment among that group and wasting a lot of everyone's time. You can find my own story about this going awry during one of my start-up attempts in the sidebar on page 46.

Exercise 4: Spectrums Contemplation (Individual)

Have each person in the founders group spend some time on their own going through these spectrums[31] and marking on each one *the perfect spot* in your mind of how your community will be set up. (I do this with an X or some other simple symbol.) Then I would *also* mark (using a highlighter or brackets) your *range of tolerance*. In other words, you might have a preference, but for most of these you also will likely have some flexibility about how close to the ideal it needs to be in order for you to feel excited about all the work of creating a community.

As an example, you might ideally want to be very rural, but could live with being in a small town. So in that case, you'd mark an X all the way over on the far side above rural, and then place a bracket or highlighter mark from the rural side to, say, one-third of the way across the spectrum.

You may find that you have no opinion or preference for some of them. That's great! Those are those flexible places where the group can decide. However, it is very important to be as honest as you can be about your answers. If you really want to live in a community that is income sharing or has a strong spiritual orientation, **it is fine to place an X and then have no brackets at all if that is really true for you**.

Before sharing your thoughts with others, consider these two questions:

1. What are a few things on the spectrums list that you have very strong needs or opinions about for your ideal group?

2. What are the things that you feel the most flexible about?[32]

Once you've done this solo, move on to:

---

31 You can find a printable pdf version of the spectrums as well as a link to an online template for them at: www.ic.org/building-belonging-resources

32 I'm going to go out on a limb here and say that if your answer is "nothing" to this question, you are not ready to be a founder. These spectrums represent a lot of different dimensions of community life, and you need to have some places where other people get to be the driving force behind what happens. Too much inflexibility is just not going to work.

Exercise 5: Spectrums Discussion (Group)

Now compare notes. First, identify the places where you have easy alignment on answers (including places where no one in the core group had a strong opinion). As long as you have overlapping ranges of tolerance, you can consider that aligned enough.

Then have some deeper conversation about the places where your answers differ. Those are the places where you are going to have to talk through things to the point where you have agreed upon alignment. Alternately you may find at this point that you are not well enough aligned to do this together. **The alignment of the core group on these vision questions is critically important: everything else flows from here.** Take whatever time you need to come to alignment or accept your misalignments. It might take a few weeks or a few conversations for you to settle into conclusions with this.

Once your core group has done your own version of this, bring this spectrum worksheet out with the larger group of interested people, sharing the answers you've come to as a core group and inviting people who can see themselves in your answers to stay involved with the project. Also make sure to let folks know that the group is welcome to answer the rest of those questions or just let yourselves default to something. Doing this well will create a much stronger, aligned, and clear core group to build from, and a better, more thorough recruitment process.

Spectrums for Community Visioning (or Searching)

Figure 3: Spectrums for Intentional Communities

Notes on spectrum exercises in general:

A common way to do spectrums when you are meeting in person is to designate one side of the room as one answer to a question or position on a topic, and the other side of the room a different or opposing one. Then ask people to imagine a line between them and to get up and place themselves where they fall on that line.[33]

Spectrum exercises are the fastest way to get a lot of data from a group of people and for everyone to be able to see that data for themselves. They also give people direct and immediate feedback about where they stand (literally in the case of doing live, standing spectrums) in relation to others in their group. Finally, they are one of the very few formats I know of that simultaneously meets the needs of aural, visual, and kinesthetic learners, and almost everyone enjoys doing them. These exercises also maximize transparency, which can help build trust.

For this particular exercise, you can also write out all of the spectrums on a large sheet of paper and give people dots to place in the right spot for them. You can use color coding for this if it is important to distinguish between different people's input. For starting groups, there might be one color of dot for people who are fully committed and another for people in the exploring phase for instance. Color coding adds more layers of data to your spectrums.

You can also do an online version of this using google slides or your favorite other slide deck application that allows anyone to edit or move dots around. This will look something like this example from one of my online workshops about starting a community:

---

33 Accessibility Note: when doing these exercises live, as described above, you MUST check for mobility challenges with this, and adapt as necessary to make sure everyone can participate. A beach ball or chair can be good "stand-ins" for someone who can't stand for very long or not at all, and someone can be assigned to move the stand-in for them. Other considerations are making sure people can hear/interpret the facilitator and conversations, and that people have time to understand and process the options before they choose their place on the line.

EXAMPLE: What's your vision? Economic Model

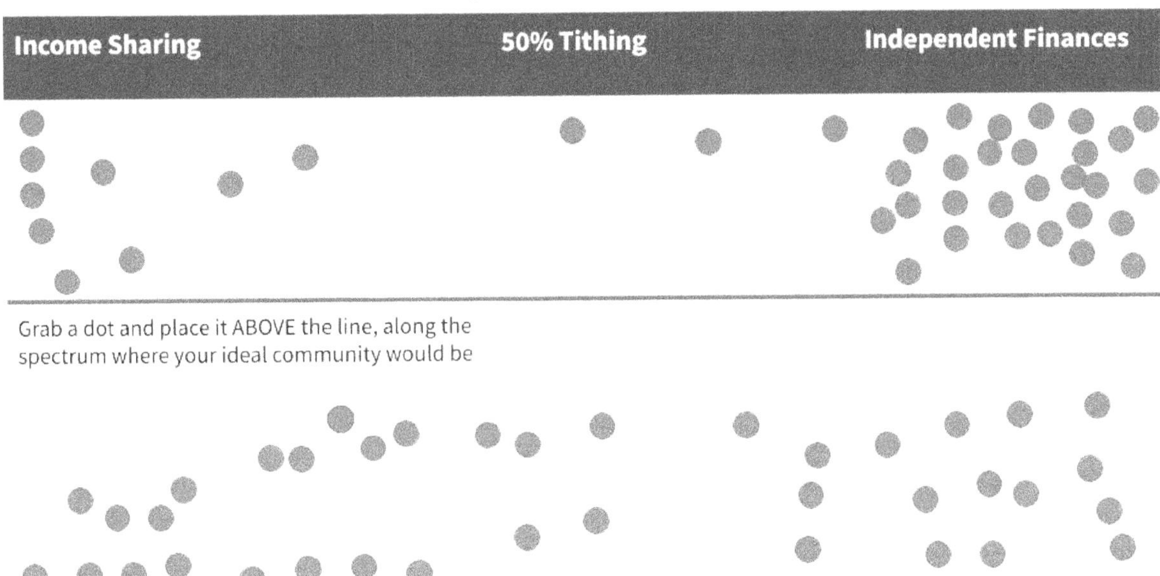

Figure 4: Online Spectrums Example

Here are a couple additional variations you can play with:

1. Moving Spectrums. While people usually stay where they initially placed themselves on the spectrum for some discussion, you can explicitly invite people to move in response to other people's statements. This gives people real-time feedback on how their words are affecting other people's perspectives. It also gives people permission to change. Both of those things are good training exercises for living together: both receiving feedback and changing our minds are things we need to get good at.

2. Grid or Two-Dimensional Spectrums. This variation has two axes to it, so that you end up with four quadrants that people can place themselves in. (Note: you need a pretty big room to pull this one off!) It is a good idea to ask one question, let people settle in, and then ask the second question, rather than give them both at once. Some examples of labels for the second axis that you would add to a first question include:

    a. How long people have been in the group. This is often revealing of patterns that can show how well the group is orienting newer folks into the mix.

b. How important this topic or issue is for them.

c. Level of discretionary income each person has — which is helpful for anything that has budgetary implications to reveal any class biases your ideas may be embodying.

A little more about the online version of spectrum exercises.

Like the example shared, you can do spectrums online with a combination of Zoom and Google Slides or Miro (or similar platforms). Create spectrum slides ahead of time. Have enough dots also prepared so that everyone gets a dot. Give everyone "edit" permission, and demonstrate for them clicking, dragging, and dropping a dot into position. Color coding dots can help you gather even more information and serve a similar purpose as the Two Dimensional spectrums for live meetings. Small squares with initials can also be used if it is helpful in some way to track individual responses.

Hint: Practicing with a light or fun topic is useful the first time you use this, especially if members of your group are less comfortable with tech. The facilitator can also move dots for people if there is a tech barrier to participating.

Facilitative notes on spectrums of any style:

One of the most interesting moments in a spectrum exercise is when someone resists the instructions. They don't like the either/or feeling of the set-up, or want to stand in multiple places at once, or simply don't like the ends you chose. This kind of rebellion is actually great! It's a sign of trust and a pathway to claiming their voice for the individual in this moment if the facilitator (and group in general) respond well. Remember that *everything that happens during a spectrum exercise is* **data** in some form or another. Welcome this kind of resistance and get curious: some of the most useful information on a spectrum is revealed in these moments.

You also might want to pay attention to whether there are demographic clusters in the answers people are giving you. If all the white people or men or all the working class people are bunched up together with everyone else spread out (or a barbell forms with clear demographic differences in position), it's worth getting under the surface for why. This can be a good way to identify places where you might be building in normative and exclusionary assumptions to your systems by making certain choices. Take these observations seriously and practice non-shaming facilitation of "outliers."

One final tool:

Another framework I have found helpful is from the Gaia Education curriculum created by the Global Ecovillage Network. Though they have done multiple iterations of the curriculum and core framework over the years, all of them portray sustainability as having multiple "dimensions" rather than just being a physical outcome. The simplest version is this four-part graphic.[34] Whether you see your group being an ecovillage or not, spending a little time contemplating what should be in your vision that addresses each of these four areas is a valuable check in. I share it here out of deep respect for the work the Global Ecovillage Network has done over the years. Because their work transcended the boundaries of language, culture, climate, and geography, I believe it passes the test for being a universally valuable framework.

Ecovillage Design Education examines 4 Dimensions of Sustainability through a Whole Systems approach

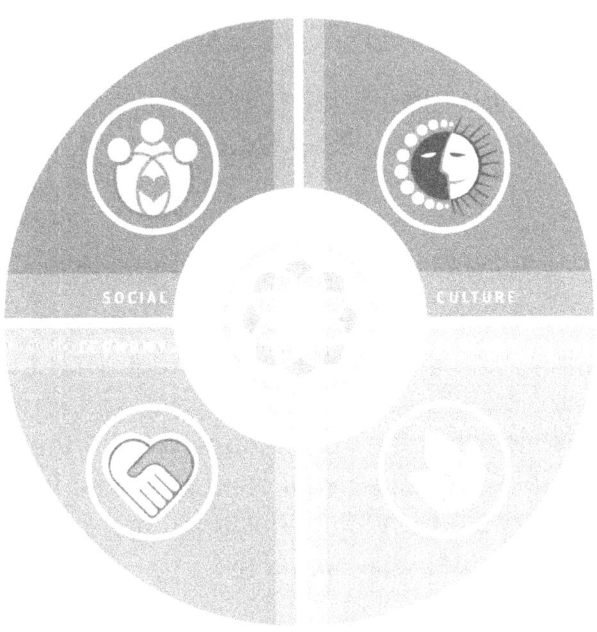

Figure 5: Dimensions of Sustainability credit: the Gaia Education Curriculum

---

34 What is labeled "culture" in this current version has sometimes been called "worldview," and I actually find that language a little more useful for visioning. Your vision is, in some ways, the worldview of your project — the lens through which you will see all of your work that defines the "why" of the project. Social, economic, and ecological aspects of your project ideally flow from the vision.

Here's some very different examples of really good mission statements.

These were all pulled from public sources in 2021 or 2022. They may have evolved since then, so please pay attention to what they now say and not hold any of these groups to this one moment in time if you interact with them. They are here because I really like how they put things together in this iteration, but they absolutely get to change their minds.

Soul Fire Farm, Petersburg, NY:

Soul Fire Farm is an Afro-Indigenous centered[35] community farm committed to uprooting racism and seeding sovereignty in the food system. We raise and distribute life-giving food as a means to end food apartheid. With deep reverence for the land and wisdom of our ancestors, we work to reclaim our collective right to belong to the earth and to have agency in the food system. We bring diverse communities together on this healing land to share skills on sustainable agriculture, natural building, spiritual activism, health, and environmental justice. We are training the next generation of activist-farmers and strengthening the movements for food sovereignty and community self-determination.

Our food sovereignty programs reach over 10,000 people each year, including farmer training for Black and Brown growers, reparations and land return initiatives for northeast farmers, food justice workshops for urban youth, home gardens for city-dwellers living under food apartheid, doorstep harvest delivery for food insecure households, and systems and policy education for public decision-makers.

> **What I like about it:** This is one of the best examples I've seen of being beautifully, deeply inspiring and yet crystal clear about what the group is doing and why. You know who and what is being centered, and have clear evidence of it being actionable. Notice that the "Rorschach words" that are in here (diverse, community, sustainable) are all so well contextualized that you have a flavor of what they mean. It isn't about avoiding that language, but it is about fleshing them out, and Soul Fire Farm does this elegantly.

Dancing Rabbit Ecovillage, Rutledge MO

To create a society, the size of a small town or village, made up of individuals and communities of various sizes and social structures, which allows and encourages its members to live sustainably.*

---

35 It's important to note this wording: using the word "centered" is legal. Saying that your community is exclusionary in one of the categories protected under Fair Housing Law is not legal. Soul Fire does a great job of being clear, open, and legal in their statement. The Fair Housing Act prohibits discrimination in housing because of: race, color, national origin, religion, sex, familial status, and disability.

To encourage this sustainable society to grow to have the size and recognition necessary to have an influence on the global community by example, education, and research.

*Sustainably: In such a manner that, within the defined area, no resources are consumed faster than their natural replenishment, and the enclosed system can continue indefinitely without degradation of its internal resource base or the standard of living of the people and the rest of the ecosystem within it, and without contributing to the non-sustainability of ecosystems outside.

Here are the ecological covenants people who live at Dancing Rabbit agree to adhere to:

1. Dancing Rabbit members will not use personal motorized vehicles, or store them on Dancing Rabbit property.

2. At Dancing Rabbit, fossil fuels will not be applied to the following uses: powering vehicles, space-heating and -cooling, refrigeration, and heating domestic water.

3. All gardening, landscaping, horticulture, silviculture and agriculture conducted on Dancing Rabbit property must conform to the standards as set by OCIA for organic procedures and processing. In addition, no petrochemical biocides may be used or stored on DR property for household or other purposes.

4. All electricity produced at Dancing Rabbit shall be from sustainable sources. Any electricity imported from off-site shall be balanced by Dancing Rabbit exporting enough on site, sustainably generated electricity, to offset the imported electricity.

5. Lumber used for construction at Dancing Rabbit shall be either reused/reclaimed, locally harvested, or certified as sustainably harvested.

6. Waste disposal systems at Dancing Rabbit shall reclaim organic and recyclable materials.

What I like about it: You know exactly what sustainable means for this group, and even get a solid sense of what your life would be like if you lived here. This is a plain-spoken, no frills, very actionable version of mission. It serves very well as a recruitment tool, as it will inspire the right readers with its seriousness, and turn people off who aren't ready for this challenge. Note that the covenants have been revisited a couple times since the community's founding in 1997, and those conversations have deepened the group's commitments, in part because the opening statements are quite bold and directive. This is a solid example of a vision/mission statement that is usable for decision-making, and has endured over time.

Brooklyn Urban Moshav, Brooklyn, NY

Brooklyn Urban Moshav is a multigenerational, urban, cohousing experiment organized against isolationist living from each other and our neighborhood. We are a welcoming and inclusive space for people and households of diverse Jewish practice and identities, and non-Jews who wish to live in such a space.

> **What I like about it:** In just a couple of sentences, this group does a terrific job of identifying who, what, and where, and uses language that is distinctive enough to generate curiosity, and specific enough to be useful. (They have a longer statement as well that goes into details, but this is about as good as it gets for the short version.) The only Rorschach word here is "inclusive" but they clarify elegantly what it means here.

The Gesundheit Institute, Urbana IL[36]

The Gesundheit Institute is a 501(c)3 non-profit healthcare organization whose mission is to reframe and reclaim the concept of 'hospital'. We are a model of holistic medical care based on the belief that the health of the individual cannot be separated from the health of the family, the community, the society and the world.

The Gesundheit Hospital Project is an experiment in holism with a medical focus, a sociopolitical act that grows out of our deep concern for the quality of people's lives and health in a society dominated by the values inherent in greed and power. It consists of three distinct initiatives which address the yearning for a world that meets human needs unconditionally: the Hospital Project, Educational Programs and Global Outreach. What started as a free hospital run out of a shared home has transformed into a global organization that is building a better future for humankind through healthcare.

> **What I like about it:** You couldn't mistake this mission statement for any other community; there is nothing generic about it. It places the project in a system that everyone knows (and many people have major criticisms of) and thus uses a wider culture narrative to create a bunch of the context for why they are relevant. It also names the specific initiatives, leaving you confident in its actionability. Finally it gives the motivations level information (quality of life and health) rather than just outcomes, which makes it more actionable and flexible as a decision-making tool over time.

---

36 I actually cut and pasted this from parts of their "about" page. This is not their formal mission statement, but could be!

Cooperation Jackson's Sustainable Communities Initiative, Jackson, MS

The Sustainable Communities Initiative (SCI) is about how we collectively develop place, space, culture, institutions and businesses in ways that sustain our communities socially, culturally, ecologically and economically. Our aim is to help stabilize rents, provide affordable "green" housing, create quality living wage jobs, and lay a foundation for the sustainable transformation of Jackson's economy through cooperative enterprise and solidarity economics. We know this is related to and will serve the practice building towards self-governance models, community control and self-determination.

SCI encompasses an eco-system of not only cooperatives, but interconnected systems. In sync with our work to build a caring, social, solidarity economy, SCI sets out to establish a Community Land Trust, Housing Cooperatives and an "Eco-Village" model.

> **What I like about it:** This is an example of a network of projects, and this mission does a great job of tying them together in purpose, theory of change and values. Each part of this whole has its own mission as well. This is another example of really well defined Rorschach words (like sustainable and community).
>
> Note that this statement is aspirational for now, unlike Soul Fire Farm and Dancing Rabbit Ecovillage, both of which have existing communities. I would expect that the Cooperation Jackson statement will shift as they get things built, but this is a great example of a pre-build, attractive statement. That said, notice that while it starts big picture and aspirational, it doesn't end there and even includes a basic theory of change statement (cooperative enterprise and solidarity economies).
>
> I also like that it challenges the reader and probably sends people scrambling for an online search to get where they are coming from. That's another thing people try to avoid, but I think placing yourself within a cutting edge movement (like the solidarity economy) is an excellent way to communicate relevance and being in touch with our historic moment. Cooperation Jackson does as good a job at this as any group I've seen.

Bellingham Cohousing, Bellingham WA

We aspire to create a collaborative, multi-generational community where we place a high value on kindness, respect, gratitude and shared responsibility. We honor each person's unique way of being and support each other's interests, skills and contributions to our community, the larger community and the planet.

We recognize that awareness and acceptance of our interdependent nature is the foundation for health, happiness, well-being, and survival. Therefore we commit to more deeply embody our principles so that we may make them a living part of our daily lives and by so doing manifest the community of our aspirations. To this end, we feel that these principles are best held as questions rather than statements, and each of us will continually ask ourselves . . .

- How do I deepen my trust, respect and acceptance of others?
- How do I bring joy to our community through both work and play?
- How do I resolve conflict responsibly?
- How do I live interdependently while acknowledging individuality?
- How do I contribute to my community?
- How do I authentically care for the members of my community?
- How do both I and my community live more lightly on the earth?

What I like about it: BellCoho gets around the Rorschach problem (which would be significant in this case if we just had the first paragraph) by reframing mission statement into mission questions.[37] They have an annual practice of asking these questions to keep their mission alive and concrete, and six years into that process, it has been serving them very well. They used to have a much more wobbly mission statement with a bunch of undefined and unrefined Rorschach words in it, and they found themselves struggling at around the 17 year mark with being unclear what they were there for.

Note: That is not an uncommon experience, especially among cohousing groups (where for many years the focus was much more on physical design than savvy social dynamics) and more spiritual groups (who can have a tendency to get caught up in very high level, "universal" language and lack any real sense of boundaries defining the group clearly in their mission work). I appreciate that BellCoho navigated the "15–20 year itch" to get a better defined mission statement while respecting their own history. That wasn't easy work, but they got something solid at the end.

---

37 Full disclosure: I've worked with BellCoho multiple times over the years, and this approach of using questions is one we put in place together. Hat tip to Damion Sweeney who introduced the concept of leading with questions for processes like this to me. I've also worked with Brooklyn Urban Moshav.

Exercise 6: Mission Statement

Once you've completed the spectrums exercise and gotten a chance to see some great vision statements, it is time to write (or revise as the case may be) your mission statement.

- If you already have a draft vision statement, take some time to assess it. Are there any Rorschach words? If so, spend some time in (deeper) contemplation of your vision work, or in conversation with the core group about them. Are there ambiguous words in it that could get you in trouble down the line? If so, flesh them out. What do you mean by affordable, sustainable, etc?
- Whether you are drafting from scratch or revising your work, work together with your core group to get to a solid draft that is between 1 and 4 paragraphs. Here's a few angles to evaluate your draft from:

  - **Think in terms of it being specific enough to be useful for decision-making.** If you had hard choices to make as a group, do you think this would serve as a clarification and decision-making guide?

  - Is it inspiring for folks who might be checking you out? If all you knew about your group was this document, would it help give you a sense of what you're intending?

  - Is it a good balance of aspirational and realistic?

CHAPTER 6: CULTURE, DIVERSITY, AND JUSTICE WORK

I've often said that community would be really amazing . . . if it wasn't for all the damn people.

It's a throwaway line. The problem isn't *people per se*, but rather the culture that we the people bring with us into community that can be really hard to shake. But, throwaway aside, I've never said it in front of a long time communitarian who didn't either laugh or grimace knowingly.

We live in a world that is increasingly defined by (and I'd argue being destroyed by) individualism, hyper-consumerism and competition. The US is, in fact, the most individualistic culture in the world.[38] Most people in North America have been thoroughly indoctrinated from kindergarten onward in how to be a really effective competitor and individualist, and for many of us there is no subculture softening that.[39] And this isn't just something "out there" that we exist within. We've all internalized at least some portion of that cultural training and we bring it with us wherever we go.

Any time we try to engage in a cooperative endeavor, that cultural training kicks in and we can throw all kinds of resistance up. There are a thousand ways we resist cooperation and back into a "me first" space when we feel insecure or threatened, and that makes creating a community a particularly challenging endeavor. So, as with any purposes that run counter to those wider societal interests, we are necessarily engaged in culture change work when we create community.

Community is not just one of those places, it is one of the most *high stakes* places to do culture change. This is because the decisions you make are so directly impactful on your daily life, and the people you may find yourself disagreeing with or in tension with in the course of those decisions are more than neighbors, they are your deep companions in a meaningful project.

---

38   Based on the Hofstede indices, the US narrowly beats out Australia for this distinction. It makes our work in community both more important and harder. From Wikipedia: "Hofstede's cultural dimensions theory is a framework for cross-cultural communication, developed by Geert Hofstede. It shows the effects of a society's culture on the values of its members, and how these values relate to behavior, using a structure derived from factor analysis."

39   On the other hand, some people do have other influences in their lives, particularly if they are from immigrant families or part of a strong non-white subculture that operates more cooperatively and orients more toward "we" than "I." One of the many reasons that racial and cultural diversity are valuable in our community building efforts is that folks with these cultural backgrounds often "get" cooperation more readily than those of us who only have white (and especially middle class) cultural backgrounds to draw on.

Successful community building requires you to *become a different kind of human.* This is some of the big work that I mentioned in the introduction under the category of "intense, long term personal growth course." I strongly recommend framing the community start-up journey to people as a culture change endeavor. If you do that, it can help a lot with expectations management.

Having a cultural North Star can help ground your work, and keep you from giving up when the going gets tough. Karen Gimnig and I wrote *The Cooperative Culture Handbook*[40] with intentional communities in mind, along with worker-owned cooperatives, social benefit and/or Agile businesses, and spiritual groups, all of whom are trying to do something different and often get lost (and give up) and take the blame on themselves instead of understanding the immense challenge of changing how we do things while trying to get something significant done.

Community is not just a high stakes place to be working out our cultural baggage, it is also a very good space for changing it. Because things are closer to home (literally and figuratively) we have the chance to apply self-awareness to what is coming up and grow faster than in almost any other environment I know. The sidebar has a very immediate example of the kinds of things I mean, a list I call "Seven Things Intentional Communities Always Fight About."

We are moving toward something that is cooperative, interdependent, driven by a sense of mission and social good, and balances compassion with discernment. This is lifelong work.

Community is a great place both to have our "stuff" come up, and to be supporting each other in this transition. I strongly recommend getting *The Cooperative Culture Handbook* and using it as a study and support guide for your community development process. You can get some of the benefits though by spending some time studying this chart (which sums up the three cultural paradigms we discuss in the book) and then answering the three contemplation questions that follow.

It's also a place where the payoffs of doing this work can be huge. A well-functioning collaborative environment builds trust, frees up energy from power struggles to be able to get more done, and creates an environment where creativity and spontaneous fun are more likely to thrive. Cooperative culture, when done well, balances effective action with deep connections between people. In order to get a community built, you are going to need both of those.

---

40 *The Cooperative Culture Handbook: A Social Change Manual to Dismantle Toxic Culture and Build Connection: 26 Keys for Groups, Facilitators, Leaders, and Other Change Catalysts* by Yana Ludwig and Karen Gimnig, 2020, published by the Foundation for Intentional Community. Available at: https://www.ic.org/community-bookstore/product/the-cooperative-culture-handbook/.

Seven Things Intentional Communities Always Fight About[41]

Certain issues always seem to arise in communities. These issues are ones where the rubber hits the road in terms of navigating a transition from hyper competitive culture to a more interdependent and cooperative one. My list (which is shorter than similar lists I've seen from others long involved with the movement) is this:

- Food
- Kids
- Cleaning
- Noise
- Money
- Labor
- Pets
- Food

All of these items have a few things in common. The tensions basically originate from these all being areas we are told by our culture are our "personal" business. What we eat, how we raise our kids, how we make and spend money . . . these are all touchy subjects that we generally avoid because they are "no one else's business." Except, when you get into community, the private/public lines get redrawn. If your dog digs up my flowers, my child is constantly screaming in public spaces, my answer is for us to throw money at something when you have no spare money to throw, you and your partner are constantly and loudly fighting where everyone else can hear it, or you don't clean up after yourself, the impact is much more direct than it is in a regular neighborhood. These issues become not only a source of conflict, but a source of cultural change because *even talking about them was previously defined as taboo.*

Because they exist at the public/private interface, they are a large portion of what governments regulate. Think about local and state laws: we have schooling and child-treatment laws, most towns have a local pound to catch animals who aren't being cared for, we regulate food safety, pay people to clean our streets, support all of this with a tax base that we regularly vote to change at election time, have noise and food safety ordinances, etc. These are issues at nearly every scale of cooperative endeavor: from what couples fight about (money and housework being top items on that list) to what major cities invest vast resources in trying to mitigate conflict and risk around.

---

41 This is an edited and updated excerpt from my earlier book, *Together Resilient: Building Community in the Age of Climate Disruption.*

Thus: these are nearly universal areas of conflict and policy-making. You will have to deal with them in the small circle of your community-building — that's just the reality. The difference between a city council regulating these things and you having community policy discussion is intimacy: it is *Asa's* dog or *Willow's* bad cleaning habits, and you might very well love them both. **Community means you can't anonymize these kinds of tensions.**

So my recommendation is this: the first time you bump into these issues, consider yourselves to have progressed to the point of taboo-breaking realness in your group. I'm not going to say, "Celebrate it!" I personally really dislike that way of trying to happy-spin hard things; no one wants to throw a party when their community hits their first significant conflict. This can be a major moment of questioning and soul searching, most frequently done in a more somber and contemplative mood.

And that's OK. It's an important maturation moment for your group, and it was inevitable.

Recognize that these tensions and the subsequent need for working them out are 100% normal parts of the process. One of these issues is frequently the first real opportunity for groups to try their hand at conflict resolution and challenging policy-making. Recognize it for being both a natural and needed part of this process.

My basic advice is this: don't panic or throw in the towel over one of these. I've seen groups who literally stop trying to do community at this point — they decide community can't work, or that the work isn't worth it. If you do give up based on one of these issues, you have just 1) let an opportunity for important cultural change pass you by, and 2) given up on your own community dreams. And that is a losing proposition for everyone. This could be a good moment to get some outside facilitation support, or even just call up friends in other communities and get some peer support.

Culture change also has serious implications for liberation and safety. In an article from *Communiities* magazine, the author describes her experience as a rape victim in a solidly collaborative commmunity,[42] and it is a terrific story about what is possible. She says, "It wasn't the first time someone I knew had raped me, but it was the only time I had an adequate response from my friends and community. Living in intentional community doesn't eliminate the risk of sexual assault, but it does give us the opportunity to address it in profound ways. In my case, my community's response empowered,

---

healed, and supported me. I actually left the experience feeling closer, more connected, more trusting, and more courageous than before."

In short, we do this culture change stuff as founders because it increases the likelihood of us getting a community landed and flourishing. But we also do it so that the people in our communities will have the kind of genuine support they need in their lives.

Comparing Mainstream, Cooperative, and Counter Cultures			
Key #	Mainstream Culture	Cooperative Culture	Counter Culture
1	Don't Bother Hearing	Skillful Hearing	Silencing Ourselves
2	Blame & Disown Responsibility	Individual & Collective Responsibility	Overown Personal Responsibility
3	Speak to Control	Speak the Authentic	Speak to Placate
4	Judge Differences	Common Ground Within Differences	Gloss Over Differences
5	Perfectionism	Good Enough for Now	Anything Goes
6	Domination	Understanding & Effective Action	Getting Along
7	Manipulation Stories	Emergent Stories	Bonding Stories
8	Me	We	Us vs Them
9	I've Got Mine	Mutual Aid	Purity Tests
10	Security Is Money	Security Is Social	Security Is Worthless
11	Differences Threaten Me	Differences Are Good	Differences Threaten the Group
12	Majority, Manager, or Owner Rules	Consensus With Healthy Boundaries	Consensus With No Boundaries

Comparing Mainstream, Cooperative, and Counter Cultures

Key #	Mainstream Culture	Cooperative Culture	Counter Culture
13	Hierarchy Is Good	Hierarchy Lite	Hiearchy Is Evil
14	Never Share Emotions	Share Emotions Well	Overshare Emotions
15	Mine, All Mine	Share Resources Well	Share Resources Without Boundaries
16	Power Over	Conscious Power	Power Avoidance
17	I'm the Best Narcissist	Beyond Narcissism	I'm the Neediest Narcissist
18	Commodification	Relationship	Martyrdom
19	Independence	Interdependence	Codependence
20	Capitalize on Circumstances	Empathize With Circumstances	Pity Circumstances
21	Skills Used to Win	Skills Used to Empower	Skills Given Without Discernment
22	Commodified Creativity	Beneficial Creativity	Self-Absorbed Creativity
23	Assign Bad Intent	Good Intent & Good Impact	Excuse Bad Impact
24	Stuck in Our Heads	Becoming Whole	Drowning in Emotions
25	Never Ask	Ask With Vulnerability	Ask With Entitlement
26[43]	One Right Way	Find the Aligned Way	All the Ways

---

43 Note that the numbers in this chart refer to the Culture Keys in *The Cooperative Culture Handbook*.

Exercise 7: Contemplating Culture

As a group, spend a few minutes reading over the chart, then discuss:

- In what ways have you experienced competitive, individualistic culture creating tensions in your group work or getting in the way of your goals?
- In what ways have you experienced counter-culture creating tensions in your group work or getting in the way of your goals?
- How would cultivating the culture in the center column be beneficial to your community-building efforts?
- Are there ways that you can already see patterns from the chart in your group? What column do they most often seem to be embodying?

Types of Diversity in Community

I can barely think of an area of life that is not touched by oppression dynamics, and community living is no exception. Any successful community these days will have to take these issues seriously.

That said, the word "diversity" is definitely a Rorschach word, and groups will sometimes use language around diversity to dodge oppression dynamics, rather than as a way in to deal with them. For instance, I often hear people say things like, "We are very diverse! We disagree about things all the time," which likens diversity to differences in thinking rather than differences in (sometimes deeply traumatizing) life experiences and privilege levels. So let me break down three types of "diversity" and my recommendations for how to work with each one.

Diversity of philosophy:

This is a type of diversity that healthy groups invite in only up to a point. Your community is being formed around a particular mission. So long as the philosophical diversity is within the parameters of that mission you are good. So long as you don't violate Fair Housing Law (in this case meaning you are not discriminating based on religion or creed) you can say no to people because their personal philosophies will undermine the viability of your group. When we get to talking about membership processes in Chapter 8, we will go more into this one. In the meantime, see the sidebar on page 71 for an example of how this can go very badly when you aren't willing to draw boundaries.

Diversity of identity:

I strongly recommend working like hell to incorporate real justice and belonging, not just inclusion (see next section for the difference). Some communities specifically center a marginalized population (e.g., a queer-, Black-, or disability-centered community), and in that case consciously constructing culture around that group makes sense. But just having an intention to be a community for all doesn't work very well, as it tends to default to the normative culture around us as a starting place for the conversation. Your language, practices and structures will be much bigger determining factors in how well your community actually works for people with a variety of backgrounds and identities. The next section of the chapter shows how you can start the work of being a community that is more comfortable for people who are traditionally marginalized and excluded (intentionally or otherwise).

Neurodivergence and mental illness:

Neurodivergence is a concept that has been developing and changing pretty rapidly in recent years. When I first heard this term, it was placed solidly in opposition to neuro-typicality, a category that supposedly held most people (the "typicals" or "normies"). That initial definition seemed to mostly be about being "on the autism spectrum" and also include ADHD and other states of being that were thought to be about the brain you were born with, and that the world at large was not particularly well designed for. For a long time I've thought of this as being solidly in the second category above, and therefore should affect things like how we structure meetings and expectations around socializing.

More recent research and the advocacy of the neurodivergent community has been starting to point to a pretty different way to hold this. While it is still about what's happening in our brains, activists and researchers alike are encouraging us to see this whole territory as a lot more fluid, and potentially even encompassing trauma, depression, PTSD. and patterns around substance abuse. It isn't just about the brain we are born with — it's also about how our brains change in response to traumatic life events (including non-personal trauma like widespread racism, the economic pressures of living under late stage capitalism, and climate disruption).

So what does this have to do with community?

First I want to encourage people to see neurotypicality as maybe **not typical** at this point. We are all somewhere on the spectrum of brains that have been impacted by some combination of genetics and events that makes living up to societal expecta-tions and norms around communication, socializing, or calmly interacting in the face of abuse and/or conflict really uphill.

When Too Much Philosophical Diversity is Harmful

I worked with a community over a few months who got in touch with me at first for consensus training. It's one of the very few times when a group said to me early on, "we are pretty unique" and it turns out they were right. They had been around for quite a while and one of their founding attitudes was that they were to be apolitical. This is a nice welcoming sounding organizing principle. Unfortunately, it backfired pretty badly.

The presenting issue that caused them to seek outside help was land management. What emerged was a whole series of deeply held philosophical differences. Sometimes the word "philosophical" is used to downplay differences as not being real or significant because they are just thought forms. I'm not using it this way — I mean *deeply held values and core worldview differences*.

They were dealing with wide differences about personal property rights versus group management of the property, ecological management (including whether pesticides and invasive species were bad or good and how much climate disruption was real), work ethic definitions, and values, if anyone had the right to tell anyone else what to do, if the group itself had value versus just the family units, what an aesthetically pleasing property was and how hard the group needed to bend to preserve particular homeowner's desired views from their homes.[44] Any one of those would have been a tough conversation; taken together, it was a deeply painful morass of people feeling misunderstood and judged.

While hyper-individualism can be hard on any community, I know of groups that have created a stable system with even that as a core principle. In other words, no one was inherently "wrong" in this series of arguments. However, trying to create any kind of policy and collective field of agreement and values had become almost impossible for this group, and certainly consensus wasn't viable. That's because consensus relies, at its core, on articulated shared values.

This was the one and only time I have ever suggested to a group that they should consider stopping using consensus. The problem wasn't inherent in consensus, the problem was that the group had no significant shared values to return to when conflicts arose or decisions were difficult. They had been unwilling to draw any meaningful boundaries around who they were as a group, and years later

---

44 If you are working with *The Cooperative Culture Handbook* as a tool, one way to think of this is that this group had roughly ⅓ of their population in each of the left, center, and right columns of the cooperative culture chart — it was a permanent stalemate on values. The right (counter culture) tendency to avoid discernment around deep values alignment and have clear mission-based boundaries is the core culprit here.

> — when I got involved — the window had long closed on being able to create a truly *intentional* community.
>
> My point is this: you might like the liberal notion of being there for everyone in all ways, but don't let that be taken to such an extreme that you are not willing to define clearly what the project is about.

And most communities are still operating out of a kind of neurotypical blueprint that, when overlaid on top of an increasingly large segment of the population, becomes oppressive, damaging, and (in some cases) retraumatizing for many people. There is mounting evidence that both mental illness and addictions have a very strong biological component, and that PTSD actually creates brain damage. We have a lot less control over our mental health status than the self-help industry wants us to believe.

I've seen groups in denial about their lack of skill in dealing with what has been framed as "mental health issues," for instance, end up with suicides, violence, and people languishing for many years struggling with addictions and not getting the support they needed because the community's pretense in this area that either the community support network was enough to help someone or that people were simply being overly dramatic. I've seen this create yet another barrier that folks had to get through to get the kind of support they really need.

Given that, I think intentional communities need to be very real about self-assessing the extent to which a group can responsibly and compassionately handle people's needs who are living with mental illness, trauma, and addiction, *and if your community may in some cases actually worsen people's conditions*. I'm not talking about minor mental health struggles, grieving, or needing to recover from a hard thing happening in your life: we all go through these at various points in our lives, and modern life seems to make it worse for nearly all of us. I'm talking about the more serious manifestations of deeper, more constant struggles.

The thing is, community is a very rough place for people who may be triggered into self-harming patterns by too much intimacy, too many people being in their business, too many new faces too frequently (if you are a community that has a lot of visitors), and too much pressure to "perform well" (by neurotypical standards) in terms of communication and social dynamics. And if the group doesn't have the skills, compassion, and patience to know how to actually be present with people, it isn't kindness or a responsible thing to invite these folks in.

In fact, this is a place where good intentions can go very, very awry. For people struggling with their mental health, community may be more *supportive*, but it is rarely more *safe*. And I have seen too many instances where someone had a breakdown of some sort, and the community tried really hard to handle it themselves, which only delayed the person getting the professional support they needed. In some cases, that made it much, much worse. I've seen groups push people with trauma into too much intimacy too fast and end up retraumatizing someone. I've seen "psychotic breaks" and suicides that communities have frankly fumbled on out of some misplaced "community is awesome" pride.

Community **is** awesome, but it is also **hard**. And our neurodivergent neighbors often take the brunt of that hard.

So here's my recommendation: take this really seriously and self-assess as a group painfully honestly. This isn't about rejecting people because they are "damaged"; in fact, it isn't really about them at all. It is about communities being realistic about what you can responsibly handle. Are you willing to build your systems to account for the neurodivergence (and let's include mental health struggles in that bucket for the moment) that most of us embody to some degree or another? Are you willing to set in place a system that can actually support people when they are struggling in a non-invasive way?

My hope is that more groups will ask these questions seriously, then decide to increase their capacity to be a good home for folks, rather than turn people away. But (and this is kind of the point of me including it here) IF a community isn't willing to make that commitment it is better to say no to people joining.

I predict that this is going to become a much bigger deal as economic and ecological collapse progresses: we are all moving into a less stable era that is likely to create more challenges to all of our mental stability in this arena, not less. And everyone needs community: neurodivergent people are no exception, and the reality is that more and more of us are finding our mental health less resilient than we thought it was as societal conditions worsen.

Groups that are built for all of our brains are desperately needed. But if that isn't your group, then please don't pretend it is.

Similarly, if you are neurodivergent (autistic, have ADHD, deal with depression, struggle with addiction and substance abuse, etc), I strongly advise picking your group very carefully, and vetting the community just as deliberately as I'm suggesting all communities vet all of their potential new members.

To go back to the marriage analogy: you deserve a spouse who is going to non-judgmentally and very concretely support who you actually are, rather than some fantasy of normative psychology. Not all groups are going to be able to pull that off, but some can for sure. I've experienced being part of a group that understands the prevalence of mental health struggles, where all of us were able to own our real experiences and differences, and talk about it openly, and it was an absolute lifeline for me and other people in that group.

Community Isn't Enough to Heal Trauma

Guest contribution by Matt Stannard

Intentional community offers the potential for living in contexts high in trust, intimate communication, and resource-sharing. All of these should ideally provide security to victims of trauma and abuse. But it's not that simple, and there are many reasons living in community might make survivors feel less safe, not more. Community members may celebrate the resilience of trauma survivors, but unintentionally turn that celebration into an expectation that survivors be strong *when we want them to be*. Here are three important things to remember about trauma and intentional community:

1. Some practices and policies that make sense to the community can be threatening to trauma survivors.

A community's policy of prohibiting individual car ownership makes tons of sense from ecological and communitarian perspectives. But survivors of abuse may view their ability to drive away from a bad situation as essential for their security, and don't want to depend on a community vehicle to be able to do it. Or consider many communities' use of various deep communication methods ("circling," "deep check-ins," etc.). These practices might summon feelings and experiences abuse survivors are not ready to process or share.

2. An intentional community isn't a hospital, and a communal activist is not a doctor.

Intentional communities also attract practitioners of myriad methods of decision making, conflict resolution, and even mental and emotional healing. But training in those methods, and the ability to teach them to others, doesn't make one a *trained or licensed clinician* unless it actually does. Being able to teach relational skills doesn't make one a licensed psychologist any more than learning basic first aid to respond to a cut on someone's leg makes one a brain surgeon.

3. Communities must be willing to ride the uncertainty with survivors.

To understand trauma[45] is to understand that "fixing" that trauma is often beyond the capacity of most people and projects in everyday life, even in your wonderful community. While the survivor can help others understand abuse and oppression, and thus help lay the groundwork to transcend it, *community members must never expect such resources from the survivor as a matter of course.* Sometimes they can do it, sometimes they can't. Also, community members must never question a survivor's preference to have a way out — a back door, an escape route or safe zone, not subject to arbitration or approval by the community in any way.

Resilience isn't a thing — it's not a set of tools or pills. As Mary R. Harvey writes,[46] "resilience is *transactional* in nature" [emphasis added]. Communities must negotiate their spaces with trauma survivors rather than expecting those places to be ready-made or easily adapted into. There are directions, but there are no "solutions" in the sense of finality. Trauma-informed community accepts such ambiguity and commits to helping trauma survivors feel safe in shared spaces where everyone accepts that we can't fix everything and we don't always know what's going on.

Focus on justice and belonging, not inclusion:

Let's start with a few descriptions of what I mean by those terms:

Inclusion implies someone different from the group norm being added to an already existing system. Simply being included doesn't tell you anything about how or if genuine needs are met. And if the table is already set before someone is included, the assumptions of the table-setters will be considered normal. Inclusion talks often about a "level playing field," operates based on invitations that are comfortable for the people defined as the norm, and don't necessarily rock the existing boat. Inclusion sees *the work of being a diverse group as being on marginalized people to fit in.*

Justice is context-laden. It balances both subjective, individual experiences with objective, societal realities. It implies partnership in setting the table, and includes recognition of historical oppression dynamics that the group can become a vehicle for either replicating, or dismantling and repairing the harm that has happened. *Justice sees liberation and the work of being a diverse group as everyone's work and to*

45   https://www.uoguelph.ca/arts/sites/uoguelph.ca.arts/files/public/FreedmanPsychicTrauma.pdf.

46   https://nursingacademy.com/wp-content/uploads/2020/01/ecologicalunderstandingharvey.pdf.

everyone's benefit. In a justice-based system, the dominant group is willing to endure discomfort, challenge, and growth in order for it to truly be everyone's group, and take significant responsibility for their self-education toward that end.

Belonging is, I think, the real goal for a lot of groups. Belonging means that your whole self is welcome here. You do not have to act a certain way to fit in. If how you show up is new or different for me, I'm going to be present with you and learn from you, rather than try to make you into someone who is comfortable for me. Belonging is largely about never being asked to check a part of yourself at the door. If that is the goal, everyone benefits, even if not everyone is equally comfortable in the process.

Unpacking Privilege

You may be wondering why I'm so focused on oppression dynamics in this book. This might be a good time to share this quote from Sky Blue (the white former Executive Director of FIC and a long time colleague of mine) to help give some context for why someone who works at the movement level would think this is so important to include in a book about the forming of single communities.

> "Accessing all the different kinds of resources necessary to start intentional communities takes privilege and is more accessible to white people. When white people start intentional communities they are going to make them, even if unintentionally, so that they are more comfortable to other white people. They are also going to face less discrimination and hostility and be more likely to broadcast their presence. As communities start networking, it's going to tend to be white communities that connect with each other and support each other. And when organizations start forming out of this network, it's going to be white people who end up in leadership positions. This means that the movement is going to focus on the concerns of white people. It's the experiences and stories of white people that define what the movement is about, and this is going to be a self-reinforcing dynamic.
>
> "This is what's happened, and this is white supremacy in action."

Privilege manifests as comfort, familiarity, not having to question things or stretch, and less struggle. It is closely related to what is considered normal or normative. (So whiteness is treated as normative, and you will hear the phrase "white privilege.") When you have it, you rarely see it . . . and may be using it inappropriately without realizing it. When you don't have it, it is often glaringly obvious. You can have privilege in some ways and not others *in the same situation*. Poor white people have racial privilege, but not economic privilege, for instance. Having some forms of privilege does not mean your life is easy: *it means you are not struggling more because of some parts of yourself.*

Every decision, structure, meeting format choice and system works better for some people than others. These are concrete expressions of privilege. In other words, every choice we make privileges someone. **In order to do deep and real diversity work, the constant question is, "Who or what does this thing privilege?"**

I want you to ask this question because of what Sky is talking about above. When we aren't vigilant about how privilege is playing out, we build supremacies into our systems, and when that gets aggregated across the movement, we have a movement with supremacies built into them. And that means that all the genuine benefits of diversity — the ways we think differently, relate differently, hold culture differently are going to get lost. And it means that only a certain subset of people can access all the benefits of living communally.

Privilege can be confusing and tricky to sort through because it often manifests as a mixture of things that everyone should have, and things no one should have. Here's a VERY partial list of "shoulds" and "should nots."

Learning What Justice Means

In my early days of anti-racism work, one of the exercises a group of white folks did together was spend time considering how a world without racism would benefit each of us. It was an enlightening experience, and one that helped all of us shift from white saviorism and thinking we were doing work on racism *for* BIPOC folks, to a justice framework that allowed us to start experiencing solidarity.

That same exercise can be used for any identity where you are in the oppressor group — heterosexual people can ask how a world without homophobia would benefit them, men can ask how a world without sexism would benefit them, etc.

A few years later, I had my first exposure to Tema Okun's work on White Supremacy Culture,[1] and I highly recommend groups check out their work. Interestingly enough, the "antidotes" they describe to white supremacy culture have a LOT in common with the kind of culture many of us long for in our community lives. Embracing this and other work to undo supremacies is some of the most direct work we can all do to end up with communities that really do work for a much bigger group of people . . . and for the world.

---

1   https://www.whitesupremacyculture.info/characteristics.html.

Everyone should have (and people without privilege often don't have):

- Good housing and food
- Clean water and air
- Self-determination
- Control over their own bodies
- Work (or other ways to contribute) that is fulfilling
- The right to be heard and taken into account
- Safety in their home and on the streets
- Their knowledge respected and stories about their experience believed
- Influence on decisions that affect their lives
- Group process that works well for their minds and learning styles

No one should have (and people with privilege often have):

- Control over other's bodies
- The right to comfort *at the expense of others*
- Unquestioned authority on things they know little about
- The ability to get away with harming others without consequence or to be able to buy their way out of consequences
- Economic and legal structures that protect their interests against others
- People unconsciously assuming they are better than others
- The right to interrupt or shut down others in meetings

Some community-relevant examples of privilege everyone should have:

- Having group process that fits well with my communication and learning style a significant portion of the time
- Being able to get into the building where meetings are held, and the room arranged in a way that allows for my full participation
- Having my work schedule taken into account when scheduling both meetings and the fun stuff
- Having "affordability" defined in a way that works for someone working at a low to mid-wage job, without a partner making more money
- The community offering childcare for important events
- The community taking responsibility to self-educate about oppression of people like me, rather than me having to fight for it
- Having someone else interrupt someone shutting down people like me

Exercise 8: Privilege in my life

What privilege do you have and how may it have made your life easier (even if it has been hard)? Can you feel the difference between an area of life where you do have privilege and one where you don't?

Exercise 9: Who do we privilege?

- Who or what does our group privilege? Ask this question generally, but then also take time to assess it in terms of particular groups of people. For instance, do we operate in ways that make it really hard for people with disabilities to participate? Have Black people come and gone, and what might it be about us that is generating that pattern?
- How comfortable are our meetings for neurodivergent folks?
- Are communication styles from different cultural backgrounds acceptable in our meetings? Are there voices regularly not heard in our community process? Have we done things to set that up? How can we become more genuinely equitable?
- Are there societal or historical injustices our community can be a vehicle to change? Or are we simply recreating them on a small scale?
- What interests do our economic and legal structures protect? At whose expense?

Repeat the above contemplation regularly, and as the group expands, include more people in the conversation.

At the core of the questions in this chapter is, "Who or what are our community building efforts for?" If our answers are in any way about benefiting the world at large, then we can't dodge these sticky questions about culture and diversity. Knowing that this stuff can feel really challenging, there are more exercises in *The Cooperative Culture Handbook,* including "8-Minute Life Stories" and the "Privilege Walk."[47] They are designed to gently draw out perspectives the group will benefit from on privilege and oppression dynamics.

---

47   The full original version can be found here: https://studentaffairs.psu.edu/learningmodules/powerworkshop/privilegewalk.shtml.

CHAPTER 7: POWER, CONFLICT, AND DECISION-MAKING

Working on this book about starting residential communities, and one of the things that has been dancing around the edges of my brain is how much the nature of organizations is defined first and foremost by how we orient to power. Founders have a really tricky role once things are established.

— Me, on Facebook,
the day before this book was due to my editor

Whole books are written on power, many of them teaching people how to get more of it, and defining it in line with mainstream culture: domination, winning, and individual interests being served. Starhawk's book *The Empowerment Manual*[48] is a good example of someone who has articulated a healthy vision of power, influenced in part by living in community for many years, as well as political organizing.

For me, power is the ability to get things done or stop them from getting done. It is neither good nor bad by itself, but it is deeply impactful on our relationships. Power is present in all relationships, and embedded in every policy conversation, work party, and meeting we participate in. How we orient to and define power matters, and the beliefs we have about power follow us into every group we become part of. That is no less true in our intentional community spaces than it is in organizing work.

But here's the thing: power is necessary for us to get anything done. Being power avoidant means relegating our community dreams to dream-land permanently.

Unfortunately, power is a taboo subject in most intentional communities (other than the gossip mill), and the inability to talk about power is a problem.

I've been using an exercise called 101 Ways to Get Power in a Group[49] for about a decade now. It is always interesting to unpack the ways we each wield and give into power, and which manifestations of it each of us sees and feels most impacted by.

I'm going to focus in this chapter on structural ways to distribute power, but I encourage you to also cultivate a space where power is acknowledged. We **do** need power to get things done, but it does not have to be toxic. What is almost always toxic, though, are spaces where you can't name it and be deliberate about it.

---

48 Starhawk, *The Empowerment Manual: A Guide for Collaborative Groups*, New Society Publishers, 2011.

49 Reference Key 16: Conscious Power, in *The Cooperative Culture Handbook*.

Power Flows in Decision-making

We often define decision-making narrowly to mean proposal making and passage, but a whole decision-making system is more than that. Power not only manifests during proposal making and passage, but at many other points in your overall decision-making flow. You can design organizational structure and processes for how roles are filled in order to spread power out among as many people as are willing to hold some of it. (For instance, having different bodies for agenda setting, facilitation, and monitoring of group process practices helps with power distribution.)

This may sound a little circular, but one of the most important decisions you will make early on is how to make decisions. In other words, you are setting the core pattern for power in the community. Does one person have formal power as the sole decider? Does the majority rule with voting as their mechanism? Is power held by the whole in consensus?

Whatever decision you make about the formal structure, you also want to think about all the other layers of power that interweave to determine who really has influence. Some of that will always be about social capital, but you can use structures to help ensure that power doesn't pool too heavily with any one person or subgroup.

You do this in part by distributing power all along the decision-making system. This structure is about HOW we do our work, not what the work is we are doing together. Power lives in every step. Here's a brief breakdown of what I mean:

Process development and monitoring helps set the stage for good process. The folks doing this work keep track and make adjustments when things get out of whack. When I said that every policy you make privileges someone or something in the last chapter, I meant it especially for process questions. If we are going to really have democratic processes that work for everyone, someone needs to pay attention to how that is working and be a trusted body to course correct. That is often a Process Team.

Idea or concern generation is power that everyone in the group should have. If we are not seeing creative contributions from many people on this front, we need to look at what is shutting it down.

Agenda setting is the gatekeeping function for community meetings. What gets the full group attention and what doesn't influences daily life in the community over the long run almost more than anything else. We often treat this function like a logistical question only, and while there is that aspect of it, it's also a wielding of power. These folks essentially decide what is worthy of full group attention and whose priorities get the spotlight.

Choosing facilitators. Facilitators are the guides and sometimes the control mechanism for good process within the meeting setting. I may sound like a hard core process geek saying this matters.[50] but picking facilitators carefully can make a big difference to how well meetings go, and it controls who is building their capacity and influence in our groups.

Question framing determines how the group is invited to look at a question. Are we spending most of our time on legal or contractual questions, on assessing mission alignment, or on the impact it will have on our relationships or our budget? Are we making time for more than one of these, or have we framed it one-dimensionally? What we are invited to talk about matters, and it can create weird tensions in the group if we don't choose wisely and push people into having to go "off topic" in order to address an aspect that the framers didn't place high enough value on to include in the framing.

Facilitation is definitely a power position. Facilitators decide what processes we use and therefore whose needs get met through process. Different processes evoke different kinds of data and engagement. Facilitators also often have the authority to steer toward some aspects of the conversation and not others. If your facilitators aren't neutral (or at least more interested in a fair outcome than herding the group toward their own preferred outcome) they can overreach pretty easily.

Proposal generation is a wildly different thing if it is built on top of group input, or is something we just get to respond to that one person is pushing for. Ideally, this is a place where everyone has power as well if we do a good job gathering input and asking the right questions.

Proposal passage will look different depending on what decision-making method you choose. It may be obvious to say this, but the power gap between a system where one person is the decision-maker and a system where everyone gets a chance to approve proposals is very, very wide.

Implementation is sometimes the primary way someone has power in the system, especially if meetings aren't really their jam, and doing is. They may have to follow the group's decisions, but many smaller decisions go into implementation. A person can undermine (stop the group's will from happening) or align with (make something happen) decisions at the point of implementation.

Evaluation closes the loop and brings us back to paying attention to what has been working, who has been benefiting from the way we've actually integrated prior feedback, and whether we are on mission in how we are operating.

---

50 To be fair, you wouldn't be wrong.

So why spell all of this out? The core lesson in this is that groups end up being healthier in terms of power balance when you don't have the same three people doing all of this. (You will also burn people out, because while I'm focused here on the power side of the equation, every one of these steps also comes with responsibility and work load.) I strongly recommend groups occasionally audit their own process, looking at it through the lens of power distribution.

Decision-making is not just proposal making and passage, a fall system to **manage the flow of power in your group.** Power manifests in MANY places along the way.

Process development and monitoring	Facilitation
Idea or concern generation	Proposal making
Agenda setting	Proposal passage
Choosing facilitator	Implementation
Question framing	Evaluation of process

Carefully consider how each of these will be handled, and by whom.

Especially within this context of talking about power, I recommend groups use consensus.[51] What I mean by consensus is a system that has three core features to it:

1. A decision-making system where everyone is heard and a genuine effort is made to take everyone's needs into account.

2. We agree collectively that the decision we are about to make is the best work we can do collectively to meet those needs.

3. We reference the group's mission and values regularly, and use them as a guide for all of our decisions.

---

51 More on consensus in the *Handbook*, Key 12: Consensus with Healthy Boundaries.

There is a lot of bad process out there passing itself off as consensus. Consensus is not a silver bullet for all things going well, nor is it a happy pill. Here's some clarification:

It is not that everyone gets their way or is happy about every decision. Think of consensus as a long term relationship, and expect times of unhappiness. You will get what you want only some of the time, but you should always be able to see that you are being taken into account. The goal is what is best for the whole, and sometimes individuals don't end up very happy about a decision.

It is not that we all agree 100%. In fact, if done well, you will be more aware of genuine differences, because you've taken the time to hear divergent opinions and used those divergences to strengthen your decisions.

It is not a fix for negative power dynamics (by itself). Consensus helps distribute power. So does tending to the whole decision-making system as I described earlier. So does good conflict resolution and being open to talking about power and oppression dynamics. So does everyone leaning into the purpose of the group instead of their personal agendas. So does delegating power to committees (and managers if you have them) and those smaller bodies being accountable back to the full group. If you do all that, you will have relatively flat power compared to what most of us are used to. But consensus alone can only do so much.

It is not that everyone is involved with every decision directly. Delegation is a good thing in any system. However, HOW decisions are being made and BY WHOM is consensual in a healthy system.

Here's some of the reasons why I think consensus is a good match for most communities:

- Trust increases when you do it well.
- Thoroughness in considerations leads to less undermining of decisions and better implementation. It's like working the bugs out in the architectural drawing, so you won't have to move walls later. More thoughtful is generally just better and consensus holds you in the space of consideration longer and more deeply than voting.
- Consensus helps build the skills needed for good conflict resolution (listening, self-responsibility, taking others into account, etc.).
- Social justice demands all voices being heard and taken into account, and this is a core part of the consensus process.
- Consensus also takes longer in part because you are building relationship while building decisions. Relationships are what community is all about.

Within the broad heading of consensus, there are a lot of variations, many of which deal with varying levels of structure. Sociocracy (aka Dynamic Governance) for instance is a high structure version that you might consider if your group is going to be large (50+ people). *Note: it isn't a free pass on the culture stuff, though it is sometimes sold to groups as a way to not have to deal with human dynamics as much.*

A Short Guide to Choosing a Decision-making System for Your Group

Decision-making is a primary element in determining your group culture and can affect your ability to achieve your mission. Thus, it should be given careful consideration. Intentional Communities use many different kinds of decision-making models effectively: despite my acknowledged bias toward consensus, ultimately there is no one right answer for every group.

That said, this decision is not a values neutral free-for-all. I believe that the best system is the one that your group will commit to wholeheartedly, get training on when needed, and supports your mission by being a process embodying the same values your community is here for. So if your values lean toward power sharing and equity, don't pick a method that encourages power hoarding and competing camps forming.

Every answer has implications for your group that you should be aware of. The main ways of making decisions fall into four basic categories:

1. **Sole leader deciding.** Popular with more conservative and some religious groups, this is a time-tested method that works well for some types of groups: those with very strong values alignment, buy-in to hierarchy as a useful tool, and high trust in a leader with high integrity. With that trust, it gets high points for efficiency. Without it, it can create significant cognitive dissonance for people, leading to all kinds of problems.

2. **Voting (simple or super-majority).** The most familiar type of decision-making, it works best for groups with high turnover rates, low commitment to training, and a lack of interest in progressive cultural change work. It is easy to understand and often produces quick decisions. Super majorities can be anything from 2/3 to 90%. (Sometimes groups do what they call "consensus minus X number" but I consider this to be a misnomer.)

   The biggest drawback to voting systems is a tendency to induce the formation of "camps" that become competing entities, and thus you get significant power struggles over time. This phenomenon comes from only needing to listen long enough to get enough votes to "win," at which point the system allows for people advocating for a particular position to tune out and treat as unimportant others in the group.

3. **Consensus.** The most progressive, culturally radical of the choices. It requires significant commitment to training, largely because functional consensus is a departure from many cultural assumptions we are trained into in the US from a young age. It is hard to do with lots of turnover, and needs a context of shared values. Some groups do a kind of spiritual consensus that can have a higher bar to it (a sense of deep resonance, for instance).[52]

    The biggest drawback with consensus (especially if it is not done well) is the encouragement of a kind of fetishization of each person's personal needs. Without clear group values and strong facilitation to keep the group focused on them, an individual's personal thing can start to run the conversation and actually derail the group from their mission. This also relates to the oft rumored "it takes forever."

    Finally, good consensus is a terrific personal growth catalyst; bad consensus can actually stunt people's growth.[53]

4. **Community/Village Councils.** This is a variation on voting or consensus from above — rather than the full group making decisions, a (s)elected smaller group makes them on behalf of the full group. Allows for a smaller group to get both the training and full context of issues, and build rapport together for ease of decision-making, but is obviously a less inclusive choice.

    I strongly recommend having clear criteria for council members and a selection process that is not campaign-driven. For large groups that really like the culture shift parts of consensus, having a village council paired with a strong committee system where committees have clear domains of authority can be a very good hybrid option.

All that said, I believe that if you get cooperative culture right, nearly any system can work well.

---

52 Little known and quite useful fact: you can consent to vote on some topics and in many cases, that's a best of both worlds scenario. This includes things like elections where something like instant runoff methods are quite functional and preserve values nuances better than more standard voting methods, and aesthetic issues such as paint colors which rarely have much values alignment stakes but rather are based on the preferences of individuals. But it can include a wider range of decisions.

53 The most classic version of this phenomenon happens when groups practice "consensus" with little or no discernment and boundaries or reference to the mission. With that set up, people can use the meetings as a way to get their attention needs met. This sucks the life out of the group and is ultimately bad for people's maturation.

Key Questions for Figuring Out Your Best Decision-making Method

If there is really no right answer to this question of which decision-making method you use, then it becomes a matter of the group discerning what is the best match for their mission, desired culture, resources, and general population. Two main types of questions are helpful here: ones related to cultural fit, and ones related to your learning process as a group. I'm mostly comparing voting with consensus here as that is the choice most groups grapple with.

Cultural fit factors:

1. How far outside the mainstream are your group intentions? If intent is a more comfortable version of cultural status quo, voting could be the easiest. If intent is more politically, ecologically, or spiritually radical, consensus is a better match.

2. How much are you wanting to develop cooperative culture and move away from competitive, individualistic culture? Voting reinforces competitive dynamics; consensus deliberately undoes them.

3. What is your commitment to conflict resolution? The skills needed for good conflict resolution and consensus are very similar.

4. Is your group overall more rules and structure oriented or relationally and process oriented? This question is most helpful for determining what type of processes you use within your overall decision-making method.

5. Which do you value more: efficiency or inclusion? A well-run voting system is one of the most efficient for getting decisions, though you may have implementation struggles if things are not as well considered prior to the vote. Instant Runoff Voting is a variation that can be even more efficient for things like elections. Consensus is fundamentally inclusive, but can be slower to get to decisions as you are essentially working some of the implementation bugs out by spending time up front in deeper consideration. Because of this, it is often faster to get to satisfactory implementation, even though the decision itself may take longer.

6. Which do you value more: personal growth or familiarity? Adopting consensus means a big commitment to personal and group growth, where voting systems are very familiar.

Learning curve factors:

1. How much turnover do you have? Because consensus takes some training to do well, groups that have a high turnover rate (>25%/year over time) often feel perpetually frustrated. Voting, on the other hand, requires very little training for most people to understand.

2. What's your group commitment to training? This is obviously related to the above. Training in how to be more cooperative can be useful in any system outlined here, but is essential for consensus. There are also a lot of wrong ideas out there about what consensus is and how it works. Training is about both unlearning and learning and that is a multi-year process for all of us to get truly good at it. My best advice is to get early training from someone and then regularly do full group "tune up" trainings from someone whose methods and approach you learn to trust over time.

3. How patient are you with people learning? Do you have or are you wanting to develop a mentoring culture? For people who are long-timers in a community, continually mentoring others can be either tedious and wearying, or part of a long term commitment to service to the wider world. The attitude they take can be critical to the success of any group process, but especially consensus.

4. Do you have other communities near you, trainers locally available or a willingness to use online trainings and mentorship with people who are community-experienced for whatever process you choose? Regardless of the system you choose, a local mentor is great for all things community, but especially for how to navigate decision-making and conflict resolution.

5. Do you have members already familiar with the process? Ditto the above. Member familiarity may be even more critical than outside local resources, so long as those members are trusted to be even handed and reasonably good teachers.

Exercise 10: Choosing a Decision-making System

Study the Cooperative Culture chart and the decision-making questions above. Based on what you are learning and what you know about your vision and yourself, what do you think the best decision-making system will be for your group? What training will you need to do it well?

Keys to Good Conflict Management: A Very Short Guide

First off, a confession: I suck at conflict, and so does nearly everyone I know. We avoid, we blame, we take too much on ourselves . . . there are a myriad of ways to suck at this, and if your life is anything like mine, you've probably seen plenty of variations on that theme. That makes it hard to think about and really lean into it deliberately, because most of us have rarely seen it go well.

Conflict happens for a lot of reasons, and it is inevitable that it will happen in your group. Succeeding at conflict resolution isn't some kind of a test for how mature you are. We are all stumbling through this.

The more you are bucking the mainstream in how you think and operate, the more conflict you will get into. I'm not talking about drama seeking (though sometimes it gets interpreted that way). Very few of us were taught anything about how to deal with emotions and conflict in school, and as adults we've largely been on our own to muddle through. We tend to be more messy than not in learning how to express what is going on with us. This of course makes building a community an uphill challenge.

What I mean by conflict is not a dialogue or even an argument. I mean a situation where **at least one person is emotionally triggered**. Conflict always has a personal piece to it, and often there is something real and important at stake for the people involved. Black Lives Matter is not demanding change because of a theory someone developed, they are demanding change because people are dying. On the other hand, you can argue with someone about something intellectual and even have a passionate argument about something, but it only turns into a conflict when you have something at stake.

Our legal system is a **punitive model** of conflict resolution, and so many of us have been imprinted with the basic assumptions that conflict resolution is, necessarily, about punishment. Restorative Justice is a different model that says it is about **restoration of relationship, and finding an ongoing right relationship**. My work is more within that model, but it often sounds naive or feels like it lacks the retribution piece. And it does lack that. I'm interested in how we can find ways to strengthen relationships and do fundamental culture change work through conflict management.

A healthy endgame with conflict is relationship restoration and maintenance, and/or discernment about right relationship.

There is also a reason I have this in the chapter that starts with power. If there is a major power imbalance between people, there needs to be additional tools brought into play. Resolving conflicts requires vulnerability — you have to tell someone not only what they did that didn't work for you but also reveal information about why and how that affected you. This is risky, and the payoff is a complete unknown — getting vulnerable may or may not result in resolution. Asking people in vulnerable populations to get even more vulnerable is unfair and may well cross the line into abuse.

If the other person can take away your job, your children, or your positive reputation (as examples) the risk may be really big. Sometimes we avoid conflict or end up managing it in less than direct ways to try to mitigate a power dynamic. This is why processes that are even-handed and have trained support are really essential. When you have power, you have deeper responsibility around this.

So where to start? I believe our first and most important job is to normalize conflict. Conflict happens all the time, and it is an inevitable part of interacting with other humans. Our hyper competitive culture makes this worse — it encourages self-protection and being right and discourages vulnerability, which means that we often save things up until they are really bad before we deal with them. Managing conflict well is not some kind of contest or sign that you are super spiritual or something — and failing to manage it well is not a personal failure. Fear of conflict leads to avoidance, and so one key to normalize it is what I call the "early and often" principle: address things while they are small. Practice when the stakes are relatively low, and build up your muscles for this work.

We also need to create systems that support people in a non-shaming way, even if they have acted badly while triggered. When you are triggered, you can't think clearly. A lot of well-meaning attempts to resolve things fail because we can't problem solve while we are still in the high emotion: it is a different part of the brain.

Sometimes communities end up feeling like the worst of small towns — basically gossip mills — but often with way more intimate information about each other to feed the mill. So some groups try to enforce a no-gossip rule. Unfortunately, that doesn't work very well. Humans are fundamentally storytelling animals, and it's easier to harness it than fight it. Which brings me to the role of friends in conflicted situations. Here's three things healthy friendships can do to help:

1) Venting. Many of us need to be able to talk, especially when we are in the early stages of reactivity. And we need friends who will not take it super seriously or personally, or immediately go to taking sides.

2) Perspective. Do they see the same things we see or different things? Do they see a pattern in what triggers us? Do they know something we don't know? Friends can help us see ourselves more clearly, and sometimes know key pieces of information we don't that can help us understand why the other person did or said what they did.

3) Problem solving and creativity. Venting is fine, but if it stops at venting it becomes simple gossip, which can definitely be damaging. Good friends will help us decide **what to do** with our venting. Maybe it is nothing, because the venting alone provided relief, but often it isn't. Finding something positive and potentially healing to do with your upset is far better than just staying stuck in it.

Significant sections of the *Cooperative Culture Handbook* deal with conflict, and I encourage you to go there for more of the nuts and bolts (and a lot of exercises that can help). I'd like to close out this chapter with a little high level thinking about conflict systems and one exercise that did not make it into the *Handbook.*

Elements of a Conflict System

Ideally what you want is a clear process backed up by institutional resources which balance individual responsibility with collective support.

Individual responsibility includes direct attempts at good faith conversation with the person(s) they are in tension with, showing up with curiosity and authenticity, and asking for help if that does not go well.

Collective support includes having a known group of people with willingness and skill who are available to help with hard conversations, willingness to invest in training if the tools currently in the group are not robust enough, and willingness to hear systems analysis that comes out of the conflict and work to create better structures organizationally to address those underlying issues.

Practices that come from *shared* understanding and principles, such as these, will be easier for people to embrace in the moment than something they feel like is being imposed on them from the outside:

- conflict is normal and expected, especially among people raised in individualistic cultures
- conflict is not just disagreement; it has real stakes for at least some of the people involved, and undermines people's ability to participate well in the group's work
- address things "early and often," which means practicing bringing things up when they are small before they ballon into something big
- people involved aren't expected to mediate their own conflicts
- it's OK to have boundaries; it's not OK to not engage at all
- oppression and privilege dynamics are often in play, and naming them is supported

- institutional and societal power differentials make it harder for people with less power to self-advocate
- avoid labeling people who raise issues as "the problem"
- use interpersonal conflict as an opportunity to unpack systems failures and do better
- the goal is relationship restoration and maintenance, and/or discernment about right relationship

Recommended elements of a conflict system

1. Document how people want feedback.

Keep a document where people disclose their preferences for how to receive feedback. When someone has something they want to address, their first stop should be that document when deciding how to bring it up. See sidebar for some specific instructions and examples of responses.

2. Have clear stages to follow with increasing support and group involvement, and make it mandatory to participate.

When Drs. Rubin and Willis and I studied satisfaction factors in community living, one of the top three was mandatory conflict resolution.[54] This isn't a nice thing to have, it's a necessary thing. But just saying that is really rough on the group. Have an agreed upon and known system in place before you need it so that folks aren't afraid they are going to "do the wrong thing." That's pretty common and it just turns into one more barrier to working things out together.

Here's an example of a common sequence for resolution processes:

1. Try direct communication with the person first, and do your best to be curious and authentic in that conversation.

2. If that doesn't go well, ask for help. Have a known and easily accessible way to make those requests to a body of people who are willing to help, and ideally trained to do so. People who are part of the support role should do their best to remain neutral and not take sides in the conflict.

3. Create a shared understanding of when interpersonal conflicts become the group's business. A common test for that is "when it starts affecting the group's ability to have good process or make good decisions." If something rises to that level, what do you want to create as your group culture for resolution?

---

54 Zach Rubin, Don Willis, and Yana Ludwig. "Measuring Success in Intentional Communities: A Critical Evaluation of Commitment and Longevity Theories." *Sociological Spectrum*, vol. 39, no. 2, 2019.

4. Finally, as a last resort, address this in your membership policies related to asking someone to leave. That should never be the first place you go, but including loss of membership as a potential consequence creates a boundary that can be very helpful if things go awry.

3. **Invest in training and have multiple tools.**

As you can see in the sidebar, one size does not fit all when it comes to how people want to work with tensions. It's a good idea to have a few different tools that at least some folks in the group are familiar with so that people are more likely to find something they feel comfortable with. The healthiest groups I have seen usually have a menu of techniques for resolution. A good place to start if the group is very new to conflict work is with Restorative Circles.[55]

One of the best things you can do for your group long term is to invest in getting some training together. Having some practice in a training environment can help it be less intimidating. And building up our confidence in being able to help each other when we get into a tough spot is a great way to build trust and synergy in a group. Plan for periodic refreshers as new people join the group so that it doesn't become something that only the founders know or got some training in.

While most groups get that it makes sense to pay for an architect or a professional builder, there is less obvious buy-in that you'd invest in professional skill for the social stuff. But this is the stuff that matters the most for the quality of life you will create together. If you have the funds to bring in professionals, make sure your social skills are also being treated as an important investment.

---

55 https://www.restorativecircles.org/systems-and-facilitation.

Creating a Feedback Preferences Document

I have typically created a document that everyone can access at any time and that can be easily updated as needs and preferences change. The prompt I've used most frequently is, "If someone in the group thinks that you are out of alignment with one of our agreements or are acting in a way that is damaging, what is the most productive way for us to bring that to you? In other words: if we have feedback for you, how would you like it so that it goes well? The only answer that isn't OK to this is: Don't give me feedback."

Person 1: I prefer to receive the feedback as soon as possible with an interrupt or an immediate text. This potentially gives me the opportunity to fix it and try again in the moment, which helps me learn. If it's something more complicated that's going to take a longer conversation or I don't understand or am unable to receive the immediate feedback, then emailing or texting me to find a time to talk would be ideal.

Person 2: For me, I would like some time to process the feedback so for me, I'd prefer a quick and specific email or verbal input about what I did and why it was hurtful, then have a bit of time to process before having a chance to follow up with the person who raised this privately by phone or in person. I do not excel at articulating on the spot; an unexpected phone call will probably not be productive.

Person 3: Hit me over the head with a frying pan. Just call me and lay it on me if you can. I might not get it unless you are very direct with me, so no sugar coating. I might get defensive — which I will work through as I process the feedback being given. I've definitely heard feedback on my personal foibles before, and having specific examples really helps me to understand how they're impacting others. I'm not by nature very reflective, and I assume everything is fine unless I'm told otherwise.

Person 4: Make it a joke. Tease me, rib me, whatever. If you get uptight and have to turn it into a big presentation or something, I will get uptight.

Person 5: I prefer to nip it in the bud as soon as possible, but I also don't do well having people call me on stuff in public. Set up a time to have a phone call, zoom call, or meet in person. I'm fine with texts to set up a conversation but prefer to not have a dialog via text because I can't hear voice inflections or see expressions. I can tend to be a participant observer, so if I take a moment to reflect that doesn't mean I am not listening, it just means I want to be conscious of my response.

Without something like this in place, we tend to give other people feedback in the way we would want it. As you can see from the differences above, you are pretty much doomed to get it wrong at least some of the time if you do that.

CHAPTER 8: MEMBERSHIP AND RECRUITMENT

One of the most important tools your community has for keeping your intentional community intentional (and avoiding the dreaded mission drift) is having a clear, caring, and robust membership process. You can either have clear boundaries at the beginning, or you can navigate really messy dynamics later on. This isn't about what works for your personal preferences and personality — it is about what works *for the project*. Membership process is a place where good founders have to depersonalize things.

Membership is the third side of a really important triangle for creating and sustaining a healthy community, along with vision and decision-making. These three components (supported by your legal and economic structures) work together to shape the social nature of your community.

Key Triangle for a Coherent Community System

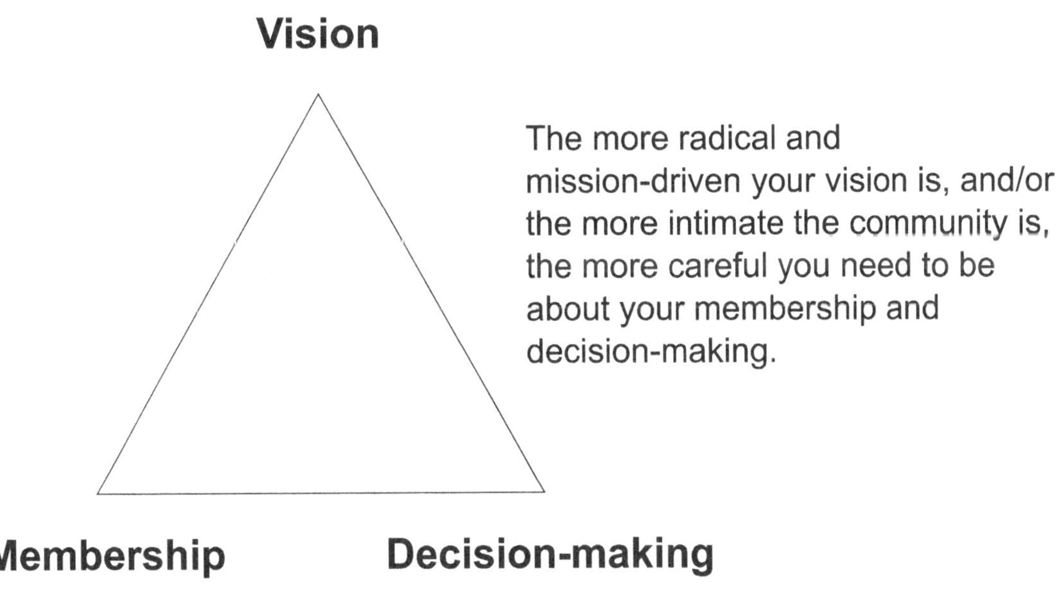

Figure 7: Key Triangle for a Coherent Community System

While every community benefits from having a screening and orientation process, the less mainstream and more radical versions of community especially require strong membership processes, because you are asking people to step into a context that is quite different from how we are taught to think and interact. More radical can mean any number of things, but definitely includes deep sustainability work, an anti-oppression or anti-capitalist focus, practicing consensus, doing deep interpersonal and spiritual work together, collective child rearing, and income sharing.

Who you bring in (or let in) goes a long way to determining how successful you will be at these kinds of endeavors. You need the right partners in the room for this kind of work, people who have been vetted for both alignment and some basic skill.

Five Key Elements for Your Membership Process

In my experience, these are the five most critical elements to include in a good membership process. These are intended to balance the needs of a prospective member with the needs of the project.

1. Have clear stages to the process. These four phases are each unique in how people relate to the community: interested in joining, provisional membership, full membership, and leaving the community. You will also need a clear process for how someone moves through the stages.

2. Pair rights with responsibilities, both of which get stronger as you go from interested to full membership. This includes economic obligations and benefits, social and decision-making rights and responsibilities, and material rights to things like access to the common facilities and being able to build, own and/or occupy housing. Clarity on each of these is valuable for everyone.

3. Have criteria for members. You know what you want to do with your community. The next step is figuring out who is going to be able to best align with and support that mission, and selecting for those traits, skills, and interests.

4. Know how someone leaves the group (or gets kicked out). We will all eventually leave the community (one way or another), and planning for transitioning out is a key part of creating a stable system.

5. Be very clear about the intersection between membership, legal rights, money, and equity. I'll touch on some of this in the chapters on money and legal structures, but you also need to put some thought into this when you are crafting membership policies so they are coherent with your legal documents, and you protect the community from potential bad actors.

Membership Phases in more detail

Phase 1: Interested in membership

This stage is characterized by exploration, information sharing by both the community and the prospective member, and giving people a chance for enough participation to get a feel for whether this is a good match or not. I liken this phase to dating. You are probably initially excited about each other, and this is your chance to spend time getting to know each other before any commitments are made. Both rights and responsibilities are very minimal in this phase.

Much like volunteering with an organization, people who show up well during this phase are likely to be invited in more deeply and given responsibilities more organically. I recommend letting people attend at least some meetings during this phase as this will be a critical part of community life for them if they join. Be clear whether you are inviting them to observe or participate (which may depend on how big your group is, what stage you are at with agenda items, and if they have particular knowledge that you think might be valuable to the conversation, and any number of other factors). Asking them what they think about your meetings can be a productive way to start to understand how they might show up if they were a decision-maker.

This phase may look different for someone who is already living in the area, versus someone checking you out from afar. If they are local you can invite them to dinner, meetings, and other gatherings. You can also see if you have mutual friends who can vouch for them. If they are not local, consider regular online or phone check-ins and doing some of your meetings online so people can join in. Once you have landed, you can also invite people to come for a visit (with an agreed upon end date). A week or two is usually a good place to start if they are able to free up enough time to come and visit.

Phase 2: Provisional membership[56]

This phase is characterized by tentative commitment, and increasing contribution. This phase is about declaring an intention and beginning to show up more as if they are headed for membership. I liken this to getting engaged. This is the stage where the community is really assessing how good of a fit this is, which means you want active participation in decision- and proposal-making, and you want folks to show up in whatever the work is of the community.

---

56   This phase goes by a lot of names including residency, transitioning membership, trial membership, and provisional membership. Pick what works for you, just be sure to use language consistently so it isn't confusing for people.

Before you are on property, work participation is likely to be committee work and planning for social events. After you land, it will also include participating in physical work on the property (to the extent someone is able). It likely includes some initial financial contribution, particularly if a join fee will be part of your financial model.[57] If the community owns the housing or you have rental space available, this is a good time to offer someone a time-limited opportunity to live with you while we all make sure we want to go to the next phase together. Finally, you want to see how folks deal with feedback and conflict in this phase. Some groups include formal feedback as part of their membership process and I think that's a good idea.

Phase 3: Full membership

This phase is characterized by commitment, shared responsibility for the project's success, and serious contribution and participation. It's the community life equivalent to being married. People should now have full rights and responsibilities, including participation in decision- and proposal-making (only now with blocking power if you are using consensus, and a full vote if you are voting) and an obligation to do their part (however the community has defined it) to ensure the economic and work success of the community.

This phase is also characterized by a sense of security for the member. They should feel comfortable enough with being a member to be able to voice disagreement and still count on people's friendship and support. They should also be reaping the benefits of economic security if the community is working on building that. This might look like having their needs fully met in an income sharing community, or building equity in their home in communities that allow for this.

Phase 4: Leaving

This phase is characterized by a formal cutting of ties with the community in terms of membership rights and responsibilities (though many people retain their social connections, especially when the parting is amicable), and mourning. Ideally you have established and clear parting agreements that include finances, rights, and timelines. I liken this phase to divorce (or widowing).

There are three versions of leaving:

---

57 Make sure this contribution isn't so big that you are already closing the door on people's participation. I'd recommend having it tied directly to real expenses. For instance, if you are printing flyers, renting space for meetings, or hiring facilitation support, have this contribution be a fair share of those expenses. I do not recommend using this as a commitment test. There are a lot of ways to demonstrate commitment, and whether someone has the kind of job that produces excess spending money is not particularly relevant to whether they'd be a good community member or not.

1. by choice

2. by request of the community

3. by death

You need to think through how all three scenarios will work. I will talk in more detail about the community asking someone to leave later in this chapter. The "by choice" scenario is definitely the easiest and really involves the passing on of responsibilities, settling up financially, and tying up other loose ends for a (hopefully ordered) departure. If the person is leaving with bad feelings about the group, you may also want to do some conflict resolution so the group at least tries to leave it in a good place with them, and regardless of circumstances, an exit interview is a really good idea.

When a community member dies, there are many layers to what that process looks like, and they are of course different if a death was anticipated versus sudden. Making space for mourning is huge, and most groups are good at this. If the community has been diligent about collecting next of kin and emergency contact information on members, it will be much easier to know where to go from here with the tangibles. You also need to have clear policies in place about inheritance, especially in communities with private ownership of housing. I will talk more about this in the legal structures chapter.

Four Elements of Membership Criteria:

Groups are of course welcome to have whatever criteria they like as long as it does not violate Fair Housing Law. That said, I think there are four key areas to think about as a minimum for making sure you are bringing in the right folks.

Values match. Assuming you've done a good job with your vision and values articulation, this becomes a matter mostly of communicating clearly and getting honest feedback from someone about whether they feel aligned, and what they mean by that. If your group has used the spectrums exercise from Chapter 5, you can share that with people coming in as a good conversation starter to see how well they match what you've decided for each spectrum. Assuming the group makes sure people are informed and asking the right questions, this is **self-assessed**.

Social skills. Most groups that get off the ground and then later fail do so because of a lack of good social skills. As I said early on, this isn't really our fault; our mainstream US culture is terrible about teaching those skills. I will break this down in a lot more detail in the next section, but for now just let me emphasize that this is in some ways both the hardest and most important part. It is usually a deliberate **assessment by the**

group, though asking for a self-assessment never hurts, and can sometimes be very revealing about both their self-awareness and humility levels.

Contribution capacity. This will include labor, time, and money to varying degrees depending on the nature of your community. This may be as simple as making sure people understand the requirements, and **can be either self- or group-assessed**. Requirements vary a lot based on the group, but a person generally needs to be able to either contribute money and/or labor. You need to take into account disability issues with this, including mental health. That said, the group needs to be very real about what it will actually take to make the community work and do your best to give people the information they need to decide if they are up for it.

Intuitive. Again, this is a **group assessment** of the person. Some relevant questions here include, "Does this person feel like one of our people?" "Do they seem to grok[58] the group and do we grok them?"

This one is obviously very tricky. Someone "feeling like one of your people" has over time often been code for racist and classist assumptions about "fit." I want to strongly warn you to watch out for those kinds of biases, and ask yourselves why some people "fit" and others don't and what we might be protecting in those assessments. Watch out for patterns. If, like one group I was part of, every working class man who applies gets rejected, you probably have a bias that needs unpacking.

On the other hand, intuition is basically a really sophisticated pattern recognition tool, and not being able to put your finger on what doesn't feel like it works for you is not the same thing as there being nothing there. I've also been part of groups where you needed to be able to articulate the reason and it needed to be tied to an explicit group value in order to say no to someone, or even ask for more time to make your assessment. That led in one case to us saying yes to someone who turned out to be really problematic and it took over 2 years to finally be able to ask them to leave with the group's process, during which we discovered that multiple people had had the same intuitive sense that it was not going to work. Don't ask your members to cut off their non-rational knowing in this process, and you will likely have fewer problems down the road.

I recommend a standard that at least one person in the existing group is genuinely excited to live with the person (more if the group is bigger than 20 people at the time). This will help head off cases where there is not some egregious and obvious reason, but it nonetheless feels off. It also means that person will come in with a clear ally who

---

is probably willing to go the extra mile to help them get oriented and settled. Coming into a new community is hard — that allyship is critical to people being successful in making the transition in, and if everyone is ho-hum about them, the group is much more likely to fail that person by not really showing up for them.

This is as good a place as any to note that collective ownership of housing generally gives you more latitude with membership decisions than private home ownership does, legally. Part of why I want you to get clear about your membership process now is that it will help you pick the right legal structure later.

MEMBERSHIP PROCESS CHART		
Criteria	**Group Role/Responsibility**	**Prospective Member Role/ Responsibility**
Values Alignment	Communicate values clearly, reference them in meetings, help prospective member understand what they mean for this group.	**Self-assess**, share how those values align with their personal values, demonstrate understanding in comments.
Social Skills	Communicate why this is important, **assess potential member,** provide feedback, offer training.	Participate in meetings and social gatherings, receive and respond to feedback, participate in training.
Contribution Capacity (labor, money, time, etc)	Have clear budgets and labor needs and share them with prospective members, provide supportive space for them to share where they are at with each.	**Self-assess**, have reasonable conversations with full group or subgroup about their capacity, ask for support and accommodations if needed.
Intuitive	**Assess potential member being careful to check any biases**, do your work around oppression dynamics.	None

Figure 8: Membership Process Chart

Assessing Social Skills

While a lot could be said on this topic, I want to highlight five skills that can serve as good litmus tests for whether someone is ready to do community. When I broach this topic in workshops, a lot of people get nervous. We tend to be really reluctant to be seen as "passing judgment" on others. It doesn't seem like a good way to start a relationship.

But here's the thing: you are going to be living together. You need to have some discernment just like you would have with who you partner with before you move in with them. You need to be willing to assess whether your new community mates are really up for the challenge of being good community members and showing up with you in authentic relationship. You are not passing judgment on someone's worth, or even whether you want to be friends with them or not. You are using discernment to decide if you really want to live with them and if they are really going to help your community fulfill its mission or not.

That said, none of us are perfect at any of these, and it is probably enough in the provisional period of community for someone to recognize the value of these skills and be committed to learning. But when you are deciding whether someone will become a full member, it is much more important to have a good handle on whether someone is doing *well enough* in these areas to live long term with them and whether they are committed to continuing to build their skills.

My list is:

1. Accurately hearing

2. Communicating what is going on with them

3. Taking in feedback

4. Non-defensiveness about oppression

5. Having a personal process

1. Can they accurately hear what others are saying, or do things get garbled?

   Invite potential members to sit in on meetings. Depending on how much back story there is to the meetings, you may encourage them to participate or not. Debrief with them afterward and get a sense of what they heard and saw. And pay attention to how they do in conversations in general. Are there a lot of misunderstandings?

Are they quick to assume and judge? Or is there an easy flow that indicates they are accurately hearing people?

This is critical because people who can't accurately hear can't accurately care. We want to be able to care about each other, not in abstract terms, but concretely. And if we aren't able to understand what is important to others, and what their experiences are, we are going to have a hard time giving people what they actually need.[59] (See Key 1: Skillful Hearing in *The Cooperative Culture Handbook* for more on this.)

2. Can they communicate well enough what they think *and* feel?

Remembering that we don't have to be perfect at this, folks do need to have a baseline ability to tell you what is going on with them in order to participate well in community. And it needs to be both thinking (analysis, theory, explanation) as well as feelings. Feelings are very closely tied to our values and needs. It is fine that some folks need encouragement, help teasing out what they feel, and a pace of conversation that works for them.[60] But if they are just unwilling or unable to be real and/or vulnerable with the group ever, it probably isn't going to work.

The group has a parallel obligation in this area: you need to make sure that meetings and other collective interactions are not characterized by running roughshod over people when they do get vulnerable. This is particularly important in areas of oppression and when folks have prior trauma that may be triggered by the closeness of community. If their only experiences with being real with you have resulted in a world of pain for them, they probably aren't going to be able to show up well. (See Key 3: Speaking the Authentic in *The Cooperative Culture Handbook* for more on Authenticity, and the sidebar on page 74 by Matt Stannard on trauma survivors in community.)

3. How do they do with feedback?

We all need feedback to grow. And we all need to be able to give feedback to others in order to build trust and have a life that works for us. And humans vary a LOT in how well they deal with getting feedback. It's OK to initially feel reactive, to need to take some space, or to ask for feedback in a different way that works

---

59 It's important to note that some people have auditory processing disorder, or are slow processing in general. It may sometimes take learning how different people need to be communicated with in order to not assume people are willfully not getting it, or aren't trying to hear accurately.

60 Varying meeting formats is something the community can do to make this easier for people whose first strength is not verbalization in the moment, particularly in a large group setting.

better for you. What isn't going to work is never being able to hear it, and using reactivity in the moment to discourage people from giving you feedback at all.

Note that reactive deflection can look a lot of different ways in the moment. Some people ignore you and go stony. Some lash out. Some go into a highly unpleasant self-flagellation mode that effectively discourages us from even giving feedback again. It's all deflection though, regardless of how it looks. And . . . it is important to pay attention to whether people stay there or shift over the following weeks.

I recommend having at least one round of formal feedback built into a membership process as a matter of course. (See Key 13: Hierarchy Lite in *The Cooperative Culture Handbook* for more on this.)

4. Are they comfortable talking about oppression dynamics as someone in a dominant group?

Most of us are in a place of privilege in some ways, and a place of oppression and marginalization in other ways. These dynamics make everything more complicated in the realm of human relationships. It is increasingly important that we be able to participate in healthy, forward moving conversations about oppression dynamics, particularly when we are on the oppressor side of the equation with our relationships.[61]

(See Keys 9: Mutual Aid and 11: Differences are Good in *The Cooperative Culture Handbook* for more tools to help you enter these conversations with more compassion and openness.)

5. Do they have some personal process that seems to help them in times of tensions, or are they actively seeking one out?

Unless you are a spiritual group with a particular shared practice that is required of all members, *it matters a lot less what this process is than that people have one.* Some examples of what I mean: meditation, therapy, Re-evaluation Co-counseling, The Four Agreements, any spiritual or religious practice that focuses on increased self-awareness and compassion, having good friends outside of the community who help you problem solve, etc. (Note: some of the above practices really don't work for some people and can even reinforce certain kinds of social inequities. Thus this list is really just examples of things that can be productive *for some people*, and not a recommended list for trying to get everyone in the group to engage with.)

---

61 For a really nuanced take on this topic, I recommend adrienne maree brown's *We Will Not Cancel Us: And Other Dreams of Transformative Justice.*

The test here is that the practice is an asset during times of conflict and stress. Any of the aforementioned practices can do this (though they can also lead to people hiding out and deflecting during feedback, so you need to go beyond asking someone if they meditate or whatever). It generally isn't up to the group to dictate what those practices are, but it is fine for the group to ask that everyone have one that works well for them.

Exercise 11: Social Skills Self Assessment

Take a few minutes to do a **self assessment** of these five questions. Remember: you don't have to be perfect, but you DO have to be working on it.

1. Can you accurately hear what others are saying, or do things get garbled?

2. Can you communicate well enough what you think and feel?

3. How do you do with feedback?

4. Are you comfortable talking about oppression dynamics as someone in a dominant group?

5. Do you have a personal practice that helps you in times of tensions, or are you actively seeking one out?

Involuntary Loss of Membership
(AKA: Kicking Someone Out of Your Community)

This is really the biggest bummer of a topic in this whole book. No one wants to think as we are starting a community that we may someday have to ask someone to leave. But you probably will, and it is much better to figure out what that will look like now than it is to wait until there is a real person in front of you and then try to navigate it.

I say that for a few reasons. Number one is that it is really hard to think clearly and be even-handed when someone has pushed your buttons to the point of you feeling like you don't want to live with them.

Second, you want an even-handed process, one that you believe is objectively fair, and objectivity is sometimes in short supply during conflicts. A good way to think about this is to try to put yourself in both positions. If you were a community member dealing with someone who wasn't working out, what would you need in that process to feel like you and the rest of the group have a clear conscience about having tried? On the other hand, if it was you who were in tension with folks and potentially being asked to leave, what would you think was fair from that perspective?

Third, you also want to figure it out now because the person in question might be someone you like. Better to have a structure in place than to have to navigate these questions of fairness and due diligence — conversations that can do more damage than good in the heat of the moment. It is better for your friendships to have something already agreed upon.

Finally, there's the good old CYA: you want to cover yourselves legally as best you can. If you have a process written into your founding documents, everyone gets a copy of that when they come in, and if you follow your process, you are less likely to end up with a disgruntled ex-member successfully suing you down the road.

I've provided a sample in the sidebar of one community's end of membership process that I think checks the boxes of fairness, due diligence, and is sufficiently detailed to be usable.

The Chicken and Egg Problem with All of This

You may have already noticed that there is a problem with my above recommendations for a membership process — it requires already-established members to implement. As founders, you are the first people in the project and have not gone through this process. How do you decide who among the people who have been showing up for meetings who the first members are? I have two recommendations.

First, develop a draft process and then put yourselves through it. This will give you immediate feedback on how the process works and what it feels like to go through it. This means assessing each other, and doing whatever tasks the process requires for each other (such as writing letters of intent, doing mandatory feedback sessions, etc.; do whatever you are asking new folks coming in to do to join you.)

The best processes strengthen relationships, and once you've been through it yourself, you will know if yours works for that purpose or not, and the stronger the relational field is among the founders, the better you can hold new people coming in. This will also lend more legitimacy to your membership status — you didn't just self-declare, you actually went through a version of the same process you are asking everyone else to go through.

Second, and particularly for groups that have already attracted more than our magic 3–8 people, I recommend doing a transparent and criteria-based assessment of where people are and collectively sort people into a few practical categories. This is the concentric circles model I introduced in Chapter 2. As a quick review in this new context:

Core Group: The people in the smallest, center circle are the folks who are already very committed. They are available for those 2–10 hours/week, have full decision-making rights and responsibilities, etc.

Participant Group: Folks who are strong candidates for membership but may not have the current bandwidth to participate fully. They might come to meetings, contribute input and have a say in some decisions but not others. Like your full membership process, you want to have in place a clear way for folks to graduate to the next circle in.

Watching Group: Folks who are interested and want to be kept in the loop. This circle has no real responsibility or rights at this stage. You might have a monthly call for these folks where you keep them updated, and they can come to meetings if they want to.

Harkening back to the concentric circles model from Chapter 2, the core group is the group I recommend becoming the first official members, testing out the new membership process as part of that.

Exercise 12: Designing your membership process

Make some significant agenda time for your membership process. Consider what phases you want and the rights and responsibilities on each phase. Talk through criteria for membership and how you will assess them. Do you want a feedback process built in? How long should folks be in the provisional phase before they can become full members? What will you do if things aren't working out (in any phase)?

When you feel you've got a pretty good system, test it out by having the core group put each other through the process.

Recruitment Basics

The principle I have tried to keep in mind when I've been involved with community recruitment efforts is this: you are NOT selling a car. This means you are really trying to discern if people are a good match, not whether you can find the right angle to "sell them" on your project. It means that if you sell someone a lemon or talk someone into something that is not a good fit, you will have to live with the fallout from that in the form of unhappy people, potential drama, and generally just slowing down the genuine long term progress of the project for the sake of a short term win. Just don't do it.

Example of End of Membership process from Solidarity Collective

Note: This is the original end of membership process from an income sharing group that I helped design. Some of the details may not make sense for all types of communities, but look at this as an example of what a fleshed out revocation process can look like.

Phase 4: Ending a Membership

While being a full member should be considered (and treated by all parties as) a pretty secure arrangement, the community makes no guarantees to anyone that it will be permanent: this is a relationship of mutual consent. Thus, Stage 4 is the Ending of a Membership.

Voluntary withdrawal: Memberships can end for a variety of reasons, and most of the time that will be by the choice of the member. In this case, it is important for the person to do an **exit interview** with the community. A person's leaving can often provide critical information about what is and isn't working in our community. There may also be agreements to be negotiated regarding finances for longer term members, and these should be handled according to our Financial Relationships Agreement.[62] The departing member should maintain good communication with the membership about their departure dates and plans, as well as their desires around staying in touch with the community.

Passive Consent End of Membership: Sometimes people simply stop participating. Members are expected to live on the property, contribute materially to the project (via labor and/or money) and attend meetings and otherwise participate in building and sustaining the community. If a member goes for a period of two months or more without showing up in the project (and has not asked for a formal leave or communicated in any other way their intentions), the other members have the legal and social right to declare their membership at an end. This should happen in a community meeting that is advertised via the normal communication channels. There may also be agreements to be negotiated regarding finances for longer term members, and these should be handled according to our Financial Relationships Agreement. If the remaining members determine that the departing members had a financial stake in the property, they should attempt to contact the departing member at their last known address.

---

62 This is a separate document that I have not included here.

<u>Involuntary loss of membership:</u> The much harder scenario is when someone is asked to leave by the group. This process is intended to balance the community doing due diligence with not having a revocation process drag on for an extended and exhausting period of time. This process is overseen by the Conflict Resolution Coordinator(s), or CRC(s). *(Note: In the event that the CRC(s) feel they can't handle this in an even handed way, they should find someone who can and ask them to stand in for them in the process.)*

We assume that members will make significant efforts to resolve conflicts before initiating a membership revocation process: the removal of someone from their home is a big deal. If those efforts have been made, a member(s) can bring to the CRC(s) a request to open a revocation conversation with the membership at large. At this point, three things should happen within 48 hours:

1. The CRC(s) will get information from the member(s) about the reasons that they feel the other member is no longer a good fit for the community. This statement should reference:

    a. our membership criteria;

    b. a pattern of broken agreement(s) and non-responsiveness to clear requests to come into alignment with said agreement(s);

    c. a significant lack of engagement around conflict resolution attempts in an area that is affecting the community health and functioning at large; **and/or**

    d. a violation of another member's physical safety, or a significant violation of another member's emotional safety, especially if it feels like it might escalate to physical violence. (Note: cases of safety violation may result in the CRC(s) asking the member to leave the property immediately. Refusal to do so may result in the engagement with local authorities.).

2. The member in question will be informed and invited to also speak with the CRC(s). The CRC(s) will make reasonable attempts to gather information from both parties in an even-handed way.

3. The CRC(s) will initiate the scheduling of a closed meeting (full members only, without the person in question) to assess the seriousness of the situation and how widespread the impression is that the person is no longer a good fit for the community. The CRC(s) are expected to represent the member in question's perspective as even-handedly as they can during this

meeting. **The only (non-logistical) decision that should happen at this meeting is whether to proceed further along the membership revocation process.** Regardless of the outcome of the meeting, a summary of the meeting should be provided to the member in question by either the meeting facilitator or a designated rep of the community, including the substance of people's concerns.

If the community decides to proceed, the following process must be followed:

1. A fair hearing meeting should be held with the person in question, allowing them time to advocate for themselves and clear the air around anything they feel is being misunderstood or miscast. They can ask for an advocate to help them communicate during this meeting.

2. Individual conflict resolution meetings can be scheduled with the mutual consent of the people involved. There can also be additional meetings on the topic.

3. A formal member vote should be scheduled on the matter by the CRC(s). This vote can happen no sooner than one week after the fair hearing meeting, and no longer than three weeks from it. Voting will happen over a one week period and needs to be advertised to members who are traveling.

4. All full members are asked to participate in a ranked-choice vote with three options:

   a. Revoke the person's membership.

   b. Create a behavioral contract, with specific consequences, including the eventual revocation of membership if it is not followed.

   c. Retain the person's membership.

This vote should be done using anonymous voter ID numbers, and the person in question will not be given a vote. The winning option needs a super-majority of at least 75% of the voting members in the first or second round of calculations. **The default result will be to retain the person's membership.** Revocation of that person's membership can be attempted again no sooner than 6 months after the vote happened in the prior attempt.

Unless safety concerns arise during this process, someone whose membership has been revoked will have one month to leave. The standard agreements for long-term members in our Financial Relationships Policy may still apply, at the discretion of the group minus the now ex-member.

After someone's membership is revoked and they leave the community, it is strongly recommended that the community hold a healing circle. This process is always hard on the group.

Some guidance for interacting with potential new members:

- **Be clear about vision, purpose, expectations and (if you know it) location and timeline.** In other words, recruit to reality and likelihoods, rather than wishful thinking. If the group is actively debating something, share that, rather than what you hope will eventually be the outcome.
- **Be clear about what you do and don't want.** If you start to get the sense that someone isn't a good fit, consider telling them that and sharing anything you know about other projects that might be a better match. I've worked with many people over the years who were in an ill-fitted community that they got into because no one told them there are a lot of communities out there; no one helped them find the right community for them.[63] In some cases, people have a lot of money invested in a community that they would not have chosen if they knew about other options. In worse cases, I've also seen communities end up in lawsuits because someone decided they'd been actively deceived. Really don't do that.
- **Listen more than you talk**, and help them draw connections or distinctions. Relational organizing means understanding what is really important to someone and working to understand how you can help each other. That might mean you discover something that is going to bring huge benefit to your community, or that their passions will spark an even deeper version of your passion. Or it could mean you end up with an amicable parting of the ways. Both are fine outcomes, and one should not be viewed as a failure, but rather a step toward living lives of genuine alignment for everyone.
- **Be consistent about what the attractions of the community are.** Having materials that everyone has signed off on and a public website with both the vision and a high level version of the membership process spelled out can help with this.
- **Ideally, have a trusted committee of people who manage recruitment** as well as orientation of new members. This ensures that more than one person is involved, and that the messages people get before they join the community are the same ones they are getting after they join.

---

63 Doing this for each other's communities and the people seeking community is part of what I think it means to be part of a movement and not just focused on our own projects.

<u>Confused Recruitment Leads to Struggles as a Community</u>

I was once part of a community where decision-making was regularly breaking down on questions that felt confusing to almost everyone. What eventually became apparent is that one of the founders had been doing some pretty bad recruitment practices.

With some folks, they were emphasizing the sustainability values and how amazing the land was. With others, they mostly focused on the potential for folks to make good money by being part of a friendly community they thought would raise property values in the area. With others, the spiritual practice support was the main feature of their conversations. It played out by having people in the same community who were not there for the same reasons, but felt (understandably) justified in pushing their reasons on the rest of the group when we were making decisions, because we'd been told that was what the community was about.

While they never actually lied to anyone (the land *was* amazing, the plan *did* allow for equity building, and the spiritual practice *was* a main feature of daily life), they obfuscated the full picture to the point that they had built in long term tension lines within the group. The lesson: be fully honest about what the project is and find the people who want that particular package. Do not tell people what you think they want to hear.

The Importance of Orienting New Folks

Your new members are likely to be a mix of people who have prior community living experience but are new to your group, and folks who are completely new to community living. I will break both of them down.

Everyone, regardless of prior community living experience, needs to know some very nuts and bolts things like who to ask about what, what the community's rhythm is (both weekly and yearly) and how your vision and values are being translated into systems.

People who are fully new to community living are likely to go through a kind of culture shock. As much as people want community, it can be pretty disorienting to have a lot of new ways of interacting and different expectations on them than they have probably ever experienced before. If you've followed my advice that at least one person in the group is excited about living with them, you can ask that person to be an orientation buddy for them. Some groups have a formal liaison system where each new person gets a go-to person to help them learn the ropes. Whether formalized or not, it's important to be tending to people's learning and settling in needs and to understand that this isn't just a simple move — it's a significant lifestyle shift for most people.

Oddly enough, people who have lived in community before can be trickier to orient than folks who are entirely new. I see people with prior experience coming in and making a lot of assumptions based on that prior experience. Make some time with folks with prior community living experience to learn about how things were done in their old community (or communities). Use what you learn to draw connections to or distinctions from their prior experience. A lot of awkward moments can be avoided by getting clear about how this new (to them) group is and is not doing things the same way as what they are used to in a community.

You will also want to provide the kinds of training people may need in order to be successful in your group. This includes both operational things (how recycling works, how to pay member dues, etc) and skills building (consensus, conflict resolution, etc.). Sessions on community history and state of the finances are also important pieces of context for a lot of people to feel at ease in their new home.

I recommend a provisional membership period that lasts long enough to be able to get these kinds of training in without overwhelming people in their first month or two. There's a lot to take in! Give folks a chance to do that and it will go better for everyone. Six to 12 months is a good amount of time to be in this "engagement" phase.

Exercise 13: Get started on recruitment

Spend some time as a group considering what you have to offer folks and how to connect with them.

- Given your vision, location, and economic needs, who do you think your ideal members are?
- What do you think you have to offer them?
- Given what you genuinely have to offer, what's the best strategy for connecting with people?

The Wait List

One final topic is important to address before we move on. Some legal structures are trickier for doing deliberate membership selection than others. If you choose one of those forms, I strongly recommend this system hack: create a wait list. The list can be built through networking, events, people formally being in the "interested" category, etc.

Have a community process for occasionally vetting and prioritizing this list, and when space opens up, reach out to the folks at the top of the list first. This helps increase the chances that you will be getting aligned people through the door, rather than end up with a house being sold to someone completely random on the open market (who sometimes have no idea they just bought a house in a community. I'm serious. This happens.)

Here's a starter list of recruitment resources:

- www.ic.org. Most members of almost every community I have been a part of have come through the ic.org website. You can do both classified ads and banner ads, but the most important thing to do is to create a (free) listing in the Communities Directory.
- You can also join the latest version of networking opportunities and discussion groups on ic.org. Lots of potential members show up in these conversations.
- IC type-specific orgs that you can connect with for their suggestions of recruitment venues.

  o Cohousing: Cohousing US

  o Cooperatives: North American Students of Cooperation

  o Ecovillages: Global Ecovillage Network

  o Income Sharing: Federation of Egalitarian Communities

- Social media pages with aligned purposes. There are groups on nearly every social media platform that focus on intentional community, as well as a host of topics that might be core to your mission. Find them and connect.
- Your own social media pages for the group. A number of social media platforms have groups where people can talk about what their community dreams are and share information about budding projects. Joining those conversations is a great way to give people a low risk way to get to know you.
- Local bulletin boards (coffee shops, food co-ops, rec centers, community centers, the library, etc.) for flyers, brochures, and special event announcements.
- Local meetings for groups with aligned purposes and values. Real life also has a lot of groups in it. Find the ones where your people are hanging out and go get involved.

CHAPTER 9: MONEY AND LABOR: MAKING IT REAL

As we move into the next few chapters dealing with money, work, and legalities, I'm reminded that Cassandra Ferrera calls this stuff an act of "hacking the privatized world." We are currently operating within systems designed to protect private property rather than facilitate collective ownership. Because it's an ill-fit with that world of private everything and racialized capitalism, we need to hack it. The best way to do that deliberately and effectively is to think things through systematically, decide what kind of new system you want to build inside the old one, and then match the available outside structures as closely as possible to your decisions.

There are three key pieces to what I call your economic structures:

1. the ownership model for property and businesses on the property,

2. whether the community is income sharing or individuals maintain independent or family-scale sharing of finances, and

3. how you get labor done and the implications of that system for your finances.

The next chapter will get into legal structures, but for now, you have some decisions

> **Defining income sharing**
>
> In the simplest of terms: income sharing is a system where all money that is made by members (through work, investments, etc) is put into one account, and all of the members' needs are met from that collective money pool. There are a lot of ways to structure it, including having shared businesses on the property and having members make income through jobs that may be unrelated to each other. It's like a couple with a shared bank account, only it's a bunch of people with a shared bank account.

to make about your values around ownership, sharing, business activities, and management of both the property and your money. The more clear you can get on those things, the easier it will be to sort through the complex world of legal structures and find the best fit. In other words, if you are going to hack an individualistic system you need to get clear about what you are trying to get to instead of business as usual.

Big Questions for Economic Structures

Here's eight questions to help you start thinking through what your economic system will look like. Throughout, I will mention those three pieces I named above (ownership, income, and labor). Answering these questions will well-position you to be able to start designing an economic system and will also help you when it comes time to pick a legal structure.

1. How communal do you want to be? You can definitely do a lot of sharing in an independent finances community, such as Dancing Rabbit Ecovillage.[64] This requires a lot of conversations about fees, and figuring out internal structures. Income sharing means having all income from jobs and businesses generated by the members go into one pot, and people's needs getting met from that pot. There are many ways to set that up, but all of them almost automatically bring a level of sharing that independent finances make more difficult and complicated.

   For instance, if we are sharing money, does everyone need their own car or can we save money by sharing those too? If we have pooled funds, doesn't it make more sense to buy food in bulk? Maybe we have enough collective capacity to put solar panels up and save the community money in the long run?

If you do decide to stick with independent finances but want to be more communal in terms of resource sharing, I recommend using the Dancing Rabbit model of internal co-ops for different purposes (including the DR Vehicle Cooperative and Better Energy for Dancing Rabbit, which owns and operates the internal power grid powered by solar and wind).

2. How important are social justice values? An income sharing system where any one hour of labor is counted the same as any other has tremendous potential as a social justice tool. The wider culture maintains gender, racial, and class hierarchies in part by devaluing some jobs and inflating the value of others. Those higher dollar jobs generally require a level of education, training, and connections that people born with more money can access a lot more readily. And of course the old category of "women's work" is unfortunately still a thing, with "domestic" tasks either uncompensated or minimally compensated. See the descriptive sidebar about one such community.

---

64 Dancing Rabbit has a well-structured fees system that generates enough money to sustain a common house with a cooperative kitchen, bathing and laundry facilities, library and kids room; a community tractor and other farming tools, and some storage space, among other things. They also have two voluntary (but heavily used cooperatives), one for collective car ownership and the other for the community-wide electricity grid that runs on solar power. So while each family or individual has their own finances (much like the wider world) there is a good deal of aggregating financial resources happening in the community. Collectivizing expenses and deemphasizing private ownership are both core principles in how Dancing Rabbit is structured. Income sharing communities almost universally use these same principles, but Dancing Rabbit stands out as one of the few independent finances communities that has very effectively used those principles to lower the cost of living as well as the ecological and carbon footprints of the community.

My experience living at East Wind

I spent my first two and a half years of living in formal communities at East Wind in southern Missouri, an income sharing group. EW had three well-developed businesses by the time I got there: a production branch of Twin Oaks Hammocks, a sandal manufacturer using the same rope as the hammocks company, and East Wind Nut Butters. Together, those businesses generated enough profit to provide all of the income needed for the community, which has ranged from 40–75 members over the last few decades.

There was also a well developed domestic labor scene, including a common building with a large, well-stocked kitchen where a team made dinner every night and another team handled clean up; a childcare program; and large gardens and an animal farm.

EW operates with a labor quota. Each week, everyone puts in 40[65] hours of labor, and there is a sub-quota for the number of income producing hours folks need to include in that 40 hours. While I was there, the income quota ranged from 8–12 hours and was revised occasionally as the businesses needed more or less labor. Some areas had a single formal manager and others were managed collectively. Labor was tracked each week, and one of the many community jobs was the labor accountant who kept track of it all. Vacation days were earned by working over quota, sick days were fine to take and claim "hours" for, and there were reductions in quota for elders, pregnant people, and new parents. All in all, it was a pretty progressive and humane system.

A core feature of the EW system is that one hour of labor counts the same as any other hour of labor. So the person managing the very profitable nut butter business didn't get more credit for their labor than the person taking care of the kids or harvesting salad for dinner. This simple principle, put into practice, did remarkable things for the relationships people had to work, as well as between people. We all got to try out a lot of things and figure out what we liked. I learned basic business accounting, wove a lot of hammocks, and worked in the nut butter factory regularly. But I also went from having almost no cooking skills to being able to plan and produce a meal for 75 people on a time schedule, spent time gardening, and got to enjoy time with my newborn son and get "paid" (credited within the labor system) for it. And everyone else around me was also trying things out and learning new skills. Without having to have "a" job, labor became something much more engaging and exploratory.

---

65 This number may be different these days. This is what it was in 1996–1998 when I was a member.

And men were just as likely to cook, clean and take care of kids, while women did a lot of the business and farm management. In a community that didn't put much explicit focus on healthy social relationships at the time, the gender dynamics were some of the best I've ever experienced. When you dignify all labor, humans become more well-rounded, and get to experience their own ability to contribute to the community in a non-coercive way (which is often a first or only experience of this that many of us got).

There are similar systems at many of the larger (meaning 25+ person) income sharing communities in the US. The details vary, but that core ethic of one hour being valued equally with other hours is similar in all of them that I know.

3. How important is it to be a full life-cycle community, where someone can be born, live their full lives and die within the community? I will cycle back to this question both from the legal and community design perspectives. It is also an economic question because having the community own all of the housing makes it much easier for people to move within the community as their lives and needs change. Imagine being able to swap spaces with someone as you need more space and they need less. No paperwork, loans, legal filings, negotiation of prices. You can just . . . switch. If homes are privately owned, it really reduces the potential flexibility. And that means that people are much more likely to have to leave their community when they enter a different phase of life. If you are going to have the housing be collectively owned, however, you need to decide that before you put together budgets for landing and sustaining your community, and before you choose a legal structure.

4. Do you anticipate having shared businesses? For some communities (like in my East Wind example) shared business is a core organizing principle. At the other end of the spectrum, some groups explicitly ban any business activity from happening on the property, or only allow for small home-office based, independent business activity (such as a therapist who sees clients in an office in their home).

If you do have shared businesses, you will need to think through a business model that is viable for those businesses, how the financial and labor budgets of the community and businesses intersect, and how to handle liability issues and insurance. You may also need another batch of start up capital for the business(es).

If you do not have shared businesses, will there be any business activity allowed within the community? Will they be restricted to ones that are compatible with your vision? If there are businesses on the property, who will own them and where will profits and losses go?

For this conversation, it can be really valuable to create a visual map of your organizational structure. Map the relationship between the community and businesses that you might co-create, as well as businesses that are independently owned and may be contributing in some other way to the overall financial picture of the community (such as profit sharing, leasing space, providing jobs, etc)

5. Do you want people to be able to build equity? Within limits? Building equity[66] is a core part of the American Dream and strongly connected to notions of security. For many people, the idea of even questioning their right to build equity is a huge stretch. But others have an analysis about capitalism and equity building that points to a very different world view for the community they want to be part of. This is going to be a hard conversation for most groups, but there are legal structures that you can choose that disallow equity building, limit equity building, or foster equity building. You want to make sure you've thought this through before you start looking at legal structures.

6. Do you want security to be defined economically, socially, ecologically, or some combination thereof? As we think about what security means, I often go back to this quote from Wendell Berry:

   "If we are looking for insurance against want and oppression, we will find it only in our neighbors' prosperity and goodwill and, beyond that, in the good health of our worldly places, our homelands. If we were sincerely looking for a place of safety, for real security and success, then we would begin to turn to our communities — and not the communities simply of our human neighbors but also of the water, earth, and air, the plants and animals, all the creatures with whom our local life is shared."[67]

Berry suggests that real security is not in large bank accounts, stocks, or even (as we talked about in the last bullet point) home equity, but things we can experience more on a daily basis, such as connection with neighbors and being close to our sources of food and water.

This is both a deep philosophical question and a deeply practical one. Humans have some core security needs and your community will be more stable and satisfying for everyone if they have a way to build and experience security. Some groups stick with equity as their answer to this question, and others open the can of worms and get into

---

66 The most common way to build wealth over time in the US is to own a home (or other major asset) that you eventually sell for more than you currently owe on the loan — the difference between what you owe and what you get for the thing is commonly referred to as equity. This gives you seed funds for new major purchases or a savings account, two things that many people never see in their lives.

67 p. 59, From the essay *"Racism and the Economy"* (1988) by Wendell Berry

this territory of asking what we want security to look like for us. Make sure whatever you do isn't just words, but has tangible counterparts in real time and space.

7. How much of a worldview shift do you feel willing to take on? I've already touched on some of this in the earlier questions. The additional piece I will add here is an awareness of what support you are going to provide for each other to do that world view work together. Will you have regular conversations that ask big questions? Will you set up a conflict resolution system in house so that people are supported in relating differently? Will you invest in an orientation process for new members that goes beyond a tour and committee list and addresses the cultural change you are wanting to embody?

The answer to this question should be visible in your vision documents, your social structures, membership process, and potentially even your budgets (thus the inclusion of this question in this chapter). What might the money implications be of your social justice commitments? Most simply there is a question of training and outside facilitation support. But there may also be more nuanced considerations — changing your world view may mean more time spent interpersonally with less available for money making, for instance.

8. How do you see getting the community bills paid? Is this with in-house businesses, optional business co-ops, fees and dues that people pay from their personal income? Each of those scenarios has implications for both money and labor. Whatever your answers are, spend some time thinking about the implications for who you will attract as members, as well as how many people you think you will need in order to pull off your budget with that approach.

Financing Your Dream

Anything beyond housemates in a rental property requires some amount of capital. That means that you will need a critical mass of class privilege and/or cross-class cooperation. Class status is rarely talked about in community founding conversations, but it is always present in them. Beyond the social justice benefits of having conversations about class, there is also a practical need for them. At some point soon, you need to assess the financial capacity or connections of your group. Are you going to have to seek funding from mainstream institutions like banks, or do you have potential solidarity support (either within the group itself or from friends and family of group members who are aligned with your vision)?

Here is a common list of ways communities secure funding:

- Bank Loans
- Solidarity Loans
- Member loans, gifts, or investment
- Member buy-in fees
- Government or foundation grants
- Crowdfunding

Talking about money is generally not very fun, especially when there are real differences in the group. That said, even an apparently homogenous group of, say, young professionals who all currently present as financially secure probably have differences in backgrounds that can emerge during money conversations. I've never met a group without class differences of some kind, and I've rarely seen those conversations be anything other than awkward at best and traumatizing at worst.

As a very simple example, imagine a community conversation involving these folks. One member has no insecurities about the community falling apart financially because they have options for moving somewhere else if it does. Another member moved to the community under financial stress and doesn't have the resources or connections to relocate. It is difficult for each to understand the perspective of the other. Some members have to work full-time outside the community to meet their expenses, while other more financially secure members can get away with working part-time, taking extended time off to devote to community work projects.

Even this amount of diversity of class statuses can distort the fairness of expected labor contributions in the community. The conversation is going to be hardest on people whose financial insecurity translates into insecurity about the community itself being successful, because they have more at stake and may well have guilt about not having this bandwidth (of either money or labor) to contribute as much as some of the others in the group.

You can make it better by easing into those conversations, crafting conversations that allow people to get comfortable before asking them to reveal personal information, being clear about **why** you are asking what you are asking, making sure class is not the only sticky topic you talk about, and providing non-verbal ways of engaging in initial information gathering (such as using spectrum exercises) that do not require people feeling insecure to get publicly articulate about their whole backstory on the fly.

Practicing having conversations about things that are usually considered awkward or impolite topics of conversation is a great community life skill. Money and class is a pretty high stakes place to start, so hopefully by this point in your journey you've gotten in some practice with this.

Why is this so important? You need to develop realistic budgets that work well enough for the individuals you've chosen to live with. And resource assessment is a key part of that. You need to know both what kind of assets people have and are willing to put on the table, as well as what kind of income people have to be able to contribute to ongoing expenses. This will be true for both independent finance groups and income sharing groups.

The majority of independent finance groups never have these conversations. Some of them never even realize that this default approach is one of the reasons why they lost people along the way who were quietly priced out of their own dreams, and that this may be a contributing factor to why very few BIPOC folks and single women (especially with kids) are not even considering joining you.

Ways of securing finance

Each of the ways of securing financing have implications to them. Here's a brief look at those.

- Bank Loans — These can be hard to get for collectively-owned projects, and if you can get them, the bank might view your project like a business, which means the bank's terms will be worse for the group. If folks are expected to get individual loans, a lot of people will be functionally cut out of the project because of racist and classist assumptions that still operate in the banking world. On the other hand, if you can get one big loan to cover all the start up costs, that is going to simplify things. Banks may also force you to overbuild (such as requiring minimum square footage in your homes that is twice or even 3X what your members feel they actually need or want) out of concern for resale potential, undermining your ecological or communal values. For some groups, that is just too high a price to pay just to get it built, and I've seen groups throw in the towel at this point if they are unable to access some of the other kinds of funding listed here.
- Member loans, gifts, or investment — Just like solidarity loans, you want to make sure you have a real contract with members who loan money to help get things off the ground. You also need to be careful that you separate the lender relationship from the membership status (and specifically from decision-making power) or things can get messy and weird. Gifts are great. Make sure you have an honest conversation about strings and that you document that. If you have a lot more resources than others in the group and decide to gift the project with $100K you need to make

sure you are doing that from a place of generosity and mission alignment, and not control. Investments (often in the business side of the community, or by purchasing an extra unit as a rental) need to be similarly "clean" in terms of clear agreements and checked assumptions about what else they might mean.

- Member buy-in fees — Most non-income sharing communities have some kind of join fee. Make sure the reasons for this (as well as the benefits) are clearly spelled out. From a social justice standpoint, I'm skeptical of the value of asking people to contribute money as a check to make sure everyone has "skin in the game." There are a lot of ways to show commitment (labor, showing up for meetings, helping find other new members, etc.) and making money the one universal hoop people need to jump through is problematic. That said, member join fees are often a solid mechanism for getting initial infrastructure built. Join fees vary a lot. For some groups this is $500 and for others it is $50,000. Again, make sure the purpose, benefits, and whether people can recover any of their join fee when they leave are clearly spelled out before you accept any of these monies.
- Government or foundation grants — This is a common part of financing for groups emphasizing affordable housing. Make sure to read the fine print and think through the implications of accepting these monies. If they are obligating you in ways that will require a compromising of your vision, you want to make sure you are going into that (sometimes permanent or at least very long term) relationship with open eyes.
- Crowdfunding — This is an increasingly used mechanism for getting projects off the ground, though dollar amounts generated vary widely and may have little to do with the merits of your project and a lot to do with how savvy your group is at playing this game. Obviously the more inspiring and relevant your vision is, the more crowdfunding is likely to produce. You also may have better luck accessing some of the other categories of support (from banks and foundations for instance) if you can demonstrate that you have community support for the project. In some cases, crowdfunding can be a key piece of making that case for support.
- Solidarity Loans — These are loans from friends and family. (See the sidebar on pages 129 - 134 for a discussion of the context for this one.) It is the way many groups have gotten established and, generally speaking, are friendlier than bank loans — if the group has the connections to find them, and a willingness to do the work to set up clear agreements with people you have personal relationships with.

Solidarity Loans are a particularly interesting option, and one that can either go really well and be a far easier way to finance your project, or can end very badly. This is mostly about the set-up and those clear agreements I mentioned above. Here's a little more guidance on how to approach them:

- Recognize the more relational nature of this: someone in the group has a connection with someone who has the resources to loan or give. This is likely to be hard on the relationship in some ways, but has tremendous potential for getting closer as a result. When I've been the one whose relationship has provided funding, my close friend and I were pushed into this very interesting dance between business-like considerations (payment timelines and interest rates) and some pretty deep emotional processing that we were both going through as our needs and stakes were slowly revealed over several weeks of conversation. There were a lot of moments for me (and I imagine for her as well) of having to take deep breaths and recommit to staying in the conversation.
- Frame it as a social justice partnership. Talk about class dynamics and power, and work for mutual understanding. This might be relatively easy if the person offering (or being asked for) the loan is already pretty savvy about this. Or it could be a really intense educational process for someone whose access to greater financial resources has allowed them to not really think much about the experience of poor and working class people.
- Interrogate traditional "strings." Who or what is being served? What is necessary for trust building and maintenance? How can both parties be humanized?
- Ask for low interest rates so the person who is offering the loan is not profiteering off the group: if they are, it is not solidarity. (*Note: you might still need to take the loan, but at that point it moves into a more traditional business arrangement, more purely transactional and less relational.*)
- Make a clear legal contract, including when and how the lines of communication will be open, when and how the loan may be renegotiated, and what happens if the group folds.
- Have regular check-ins. This might be monthly, quarterly, or yearly. The interval is less important than communicating openly about how things are going financially as well as allowing the lender to have a peek into how the community they have helped fund is doing. People who engage in solidarity lending are usually doing that because they really believe in what you are doing. Allow them to share in the wins and see how their support is affecting people's lives.

Most of these options will require you to have a budget fleshed out before you ask. Ideally, your founding group will have someone in it who loves spreadsheets and has some financial savvy. If not, this can be a great role for a supportive volunteer to help out. I've provided a resource page that goes with this book on the FIC website,[68] where you will find a link to a very simple starter spreadsheet for you to use to start putting together a budget. I recommend having your start-up budget cover not only the hard costs of land purchase

---

68 http://www.ic.org/building-belonging-resources

and development, but also the soft costs of getting social systems training and support, and at least two years of an operating budget. The spreadsheet template includes those pieces. There is also a second template for income sharing groups to think about what it will take to support your members. Your operating budgets will be a lot more complicated than your non-income sharing companions in the movement.

Community as Business

Your community will be (among other things) a business entity. A lot of people who are drawn to community have resistance to that idea. Being a *business* implies something transactional and also evokes images of profiteering. This is what capitalism demands of us, and it doesn't sit well. For a lot of us, transactional-thinking is a cultural and operational paradigm that we are trying to get away from. Unfortunately though, we can't ignore this part of the equation, as much as I am personally sympathetic to the reasons people want to.

If we don't have a viable business plan, we don't have a viable community. Period.

You will also need a business plan in order to get a bank loan, and potentially for personal loans as well. And many people need it for their own peace of mind. You may have some folks in the group who operate more on the "we trust things will work out" world view, and this will be less of a need for them. But no one gets hurt by creating a solid plan with more details to it. My intention in this section is to help you think about the business aspects of your community in the most grounded and relational way possible.

Let's start by mapping traditional business planning language onto community language.

What we've been talking about as vision and mission are basically your "business purpose" and your "product" is a high quality experience as a community member. You are working to create something that is valuable in the world and to people in the world, and you are inviting people to partake in that. You genuinely believe this is of value for them, and if you are following the advice from the membership and recruitment chapter of working to find the people for whom your project is a good match, then this is an ethical business practice.

Your recruitment process and resources you create collectively to get the word out are your "branding and messaging." One way to think about branding is that it is your repu-tation among potential members and in the wider community you'll be living in. Having a good reputation is critically important for neighbor relations and your easy viability in the area you will be located. There are some really awful stories out there about neighbor relations really breaking down because a community opted to be secretive and non-transparent about what they were actually doing.[69]

Membership recruitment and internal processes could be seen as a form of "customer relations and retention." Your members will be joining you because what you are building and offering is valuable to them. Some may be short term participants and some might be long term. A lot of groups serve a very valuable culture change purpose by having many people pass through their community over time, experience something different and then take that back out into the world. But the healthiest communities have at least a core of people who stay long term. Thinking about how to retain a good percentage of folks over time is a good thing to do. Again, it isn't about deceptive marketing and trying to manipulate anyone into buying your product — it's about genuinely offering something of value and working together to create a community worthy of long term engagement.

The things you do that bring in money can be thought of as describing "business lines" — in other words, how your business gets paid and therefore how your community is generating whatever funds you need to be able to pay your bills. Business lines may include things like member fees, businesses that sell products or services to the public, or fundraising endeavors. A lot of groups end up being very savvy about working both ends of a budget — streamlining costs to reduce expenses and keeping the needs for income low while creatively figuring out how to generate the income they need to survive.

Core Decision: Income Sharing or Independent Finances

You may recall that one of the spectrums from the visioning section was about your basic economic structure: will your group be income sharing or an independent finances group that uses some kind of a member fees system to make your budget work?

Income sharing is a topic that generally induces either a quickening of excitement in people or, more commonly, intense, survival-related fears. Very few people have no emotional reaction to someone raising the idea of pooling incomes together with other people. Income sharing tends to be very challenging for a lot of us because talking about money is often a taboo, and our North American individualism means that emotional safety is best preserved if I am looking out for me and only me (or maybe a few family members).

---

69   The worst of these stories make national headlines and hurt the whole communities movement (think Waco, TX and the neighbors being afraid enough that they eventually got the FBI to raid the Branch Davidian compound). People died. It sucked.

Cross-Class Cooperation and Land Access

Excerpted from the Spring 2019 issue of Communities: Journal of Cooperative Culture, on the theme of "Community Land."

Every community that owns property and whose "origin story" I know has a few things in common: someone(s) with passion for doing something you can't easily do within the mainstream culture, a combination of persistence and luck, and one or more people with enough class privilege involved to get the thing landed. While we talk about the first thing a lot, and the second thing some, the third element is one we either treat as an "of course" or never really think and talk much about at all. I'd like to change that.

I think it is increasingly important to not only talk about the role class privilege plays in our movement, but also celebrate the ways that cross-class cooperation can be a form of solidarity that is very much needed at this time. Land access is a fundamental barrier to many things in the US: being able to grow your own food, being able to build equity and wealth, being able to have a direct and daily relationship with the natural world, and being able to start an intentional community are just a few areas in which lack of enough wealth to own property further limits our capacity to have our dreams become realities.

Much work has been done on land and property access inequities, including detailed studies of practices within the banking industry such as "redlining" (where banks used to literally draw red lines on a map indicating where they would and would not give loans to mostly Black families) and the ripple effect those practices have had on the discrepancies between Black and white families and intergenerational wealth building. (An article on www.citylab.com from April 2018[70] called "How the Fair Housing Act Failed Black Homeowners" is one good intro to this topic.) Groups such as Cooperation Jackson in Mississippi and the People of Color Sustainable Housing Network in the Bay Area understand the importance of restoring access to land as part of an overall strategy of racial justice.

In my experience, the main reason intentional communities fail is social dynamics: we aren't taught by our culture how to get along, make decisions collectively, and resolve conflicts, and lacking those skills, lots of groups flounder. But I am also increasingly tuned in to how many groups simply never get the chance to fail because of economics. If you don't have people with some wealth involved or at least people who have done well enough to be able to get bank financing, then a lot of dreams die as wee sprouts.

---

70   https://www.bloomberg.com/citylab.

I've been part now of multiple intentional community start-up attempts. In the two cases where we got far enough along to be ready for the property acquisition phase, one of the critical determiners of failure or success was whether or not we had the presence of cross-class cooperation: Were folks with access to resources willing to put those resources on the table at the critical moment or not? In one case, there was just not enough of that to be able to tie up property, and in the other case there was. The result? My startup in Laramie, Wyoming landed, whereas the one I worked on a dozen years before in Albuquerque, New Mexico didn't.

Part of my motivation in writing this particular article is to put a bug in the ears of middle- and upper-class readers of *Communities*. Class is similar to race and gender in that oppression based on these categories needs to be addressed by the folks who have the power: you have to take seriously that classism is a thing, and ask what you can do to end the power imbalances you are currently benefiting from to others' detriment. Just as sexism will only end when men do their work and racism will only end when white people do theirs, people with class privilege are in the responsibility seat with ending classism.

I've been thinking a lot about reparations lately in the context of my own work around ending racism. A lot of folks think reparations are a fine idea but they struggle with what exactly that would look like. I've slowly come to the conclusion that it doesn't look like "a" thing and that trying to figure out "the" answer is stopping a lot of white folks from being able to do something tangible that will amount to embodying reparations. As an example of individual acts I'm working on engaging in to embody reparations: I'm working to cede talk time to people of color regularly in conversations, and I've offered to a teaching partner who is a person of color to have them take home a higher percentage of the money we make in any work we do together. These are both actions that move beyond "nice thoughts" and into starting to shift power relationships.

I think there is a parallel around class dynamics. Individuals and organizations can take concrete steps to change both the narrative on worth and worthiness of getting needs met, and the concrete deleterious effects of that narrative on people's ability to get their needs met. One of the organizations I work for, which was until recently an all-volunteer effort, has recently begun paying poor and working-class folks for the same work that middle- and upper- are still asked to do as volunteers. This is a concrete recognition that some people can afford to volunteer while others can't, and it makes possible the inclusion of poor and working-class people in work they'd otherwise be cut out of.

So how does this apply to the communities movement? In our movement's case, "land access" has a lot of overlap with "communities that are accessible" because we are a fundamentally land-based movement. I think a series of inquiries would be helpful at this time to help us start to shift away from oppressive thinking and dynamics between members of our communities. These inquiries are first and foremost for people who have class privilege now. (Note: class privilege can seem a bit murky, but if you make 50 percent more than the living wage for your area, own outright assets such as a home or other property, are debt-free, have a trust fund, and/or are secure in your retirement, I'm probably talking to you. I'm also talking to you if you manage significant assets for someone else where you have some say about how those assets are invested or otherwise dispersed.)

- Are there ways that I can embody class solidarity by using the resources I have to insure our community is financially accessible to people without similar privilege? (Hint: loan funds are less effective for this than sliding scales, gift funds, and simply paying for things you don't expect others to similarly fund.)
- Am I willing to forgo my earning of equity in this project, recognizing that the earning of equity is embedded in an oppressive economic system that is available unevenly to different people in this group, and means others will have to struggle more?
- Can I commit to acting in solidarity with working-class people in tangible ways? Examples of this are: not advocating for meetings or all the fun stuff happening during work hours, not asking working-class and poor people to pay for childcare to participate, not throwing parties that will cause pain to less wealthy people (such as slideshows about what I did on my summer vacation that often amount to wealth displays), and recognizing that working-class and poor people generally have not only less money but less "free time" to contribute, and not shaming them or creating participation barriers based on what they can or can't contribute.
- Can I commit to learning about classism and wealth discrepancies, such as checking out the Class Action website (classism.org), and encouraging my group to get full-group training around these issues?
- Do I have concrete assets that I could flat out give the group, such as land or funding for a no-questions-asked emergency fund?
- Can I consider being part of an income-sharing community where my higher wages and assets could help materially support others on a daily basis? (You can also do this at a sub-community level, such as the Income Share group I'm supporting developing within Bellingham Cohousing.)

> - Can I offer critical support such as childcare, transportation, and help filling out governmental assistance paperwork to folks who need these things in my group?
> - Can I do things like these without asking to be thanked for it, but simply because it is the right thing to do in terms of balancing the scales of justice?
>
> There are also many initiatives you can support to help us all embody a new paradigm beyond class oppression. These include individual communities like Cooperation Jackson, the Parable of the Sower Intentional Community Cooperative, and multiple subnetworks including People of Color Sustainable Housing Network and income-sharing groups (some of whom are organized by the Federation of Egalitarian Communities, www.thefec.org). Broader ways to explore these issues are by checking out the New Economy Coalition's work, and my own (working-class) community's podcast, Solidarity House, which looks at cooperative systems through a liberatory framework.
>
> . . .
>
> Cross-class solidarity has always played a role in our movement. I'm hoping that role will be more acknowledged, deliberate, and celebrated as we move forward, collectively.
> —end article excerpt

On the one hand, this is just a choice like any other structural choices you will make in setting up your community. On the other hand, I'd like to make a pitch for at least considering income sharing, in the spirit of wanting this book to support the forming of communities that move the world toward more justice, economic resilience, and ecological sustainability. I've come to believe after a lot of years of living in and studying community that income sharing is a significantly underrated tool for all three of these.

So here's my pitch.

In 2017, I approached then PhD candidate (and now full-blown Dr.) Zach Rubin to see if he had an interest in doing a study with me of intentional communities. The result of that collaboration (which also pulled in now-Dr. Don Willis) was a large set of data and multiple papers or articles, including one that was peer reviewed, published and went on to win the Communal Studies Association article of the year award in 2017.[71]

---

71   Here are the citations for all three articles our findings were published in:
Zach Rubin, Don Willis, and Mayana Ludwig. "Measuring Success in Intentional Communities: A Critical Evaluation of Commitment and Longevity Theories." *Sociological Spectrum*, vol. 39, no. 2, 2019.
Zach Rubin, Yana Ludwig, and Don Willis. "Conflict Resolution and Satisfaction in Today's Intentional Communities." *Communities Magazine*, Fall 2019.
Zach Rubin, Ma'ikwe Ludwig, and Don Willis. "Happy, Healthy, Functional, Fit: What Works Best in Present-Day Intentional Communities." *Communities Magazine*, Winter 2017.

One of the things that the Drs. and I were looking at was patterns in satisfaction among community residents. Some of what we found didn't surprise me at all — turns out that two of the top three factors in increased satisfaction were some kind of mandatory conflict resolution process, and egalitarian decision-making. As I've long held that the social dynamics are the most essential thing to get right, this confirmed my biases quite nicely.

The third one, though, caught me completely by surprise: income sharing. Given how terrified most people are when I suggest this as a potential way to structure their communities, the discovery that it is actually experienced as a very good thing by the people living in communities that make this choice was a little mind blowing.

I also documented in *Together Resilient* the impact on carbon footprints that income sharing can have when I did a deep look at Twin Oaks Community in Louisa, VA. Twin Oaks is a community that did not set out with deep ambitions around ecological footprints (and in fact was founded well before that concept was even a thing). But the level of communal systems practiced by Twin Oaks had led them to have about 20% of the US average ecological footprint.

How does that work? Twin Oaks is a community that was designed with significant emphasis on large communal spaces and systems (a large commercial kitchen and dining hall, workshops, car co-op, community agriculture systems, collectively owned and managed businesses, etc.). Like all income sharing communities, significant resource sharing just makes sense — why have everyone own their own car (or tractor or guest rooms or hospice facilities or greenhouse) when you really just need one or a few of those? And the community sees a lot of financial benefits as well in not having to own a bunch of each of those things.

It turns out it takes a lot less energy (both in terms of electricity and fuel as well as human labor) to, say, make one dinner for 100+ people than 50 meals for two people each. Having a car to human ratio of around 1:10 is a lot more ecologically sensible than the standard US ration of 1:1. And it's also cheaper — a lot cheaper. In 2017 when I pulled the number for *Together Resilient*, the average yearly income for Twin Oaks members was around 1/3 of the average income of Louisa County, where the community is located.

I have also had my own experience with income sharing, and, while I didn't understand this at the time, some of the benefits of this economic system were what sold me on community in the first place. My sidebar on East Wind describes this system.

I admit to being initially skeptical of community in general and communes in particular, but I was able to quickly see that this group was actually *doing* a lot of things that I'd been *talking about* in my activism. They were growing a high percentage of their own food and had clear systems set up for food preservation. The gender relationships were, as I say in the sidebar, oddly flat — and I say oddly because this was not a group known for particularly great social relationships in general — a trait I came to understand was largely because one hour of work was seen as one hour of work, whether that was managing a business, taking care of kids, cooking meals, or working in a factory. There was no monetary or respect hierarchy assigned to labor.

Thus there was no hierarchy of "women's work" versus "work" and people did the work they were drawn to and were good at regardless of those usual categories. And it was one of the few communities I've been part of where the type of work you did made no difference at all to your access to things like good food, housing, and healthcare. This experience remains a highly influential one for me in understanding that a world of economic justice and equity is actually possible. The implications for racial and disability justice are also now pretty clear to me even though they weren't at the time.

There are also some pretty compelling reasons to think about income sharing from an economic security standpoint. Most single people or couples are incredibly vulnerable to market changes. If you just have one or two sources of income (assuming you aren't doing the highly stressful thing of piecing an income together from many small jobs that a friend of mine calls "the Millennial Hussle") and the industry you work within suddenly tanks, your whole economic unit can suddenly lose their stability.

Imagine if instead you had many income sources without the stress of creating all of them yourself. If there are 8 income streams coming in and one of them suddenly disappears, that's a lot easier to weather. And if you have community businesses that are shared businesses, you have a lot of minds that can engage when a market change happens, rather than being by yourself as a sole business owner trying to figure out what to do. Either way, you are going to be a lot better off when things change.

My point is basically this: if your community has goals around justice, economic resilience, or sustainability, income sharing is one tool that makes a lot of good decisions no-brainers. (Remember, Twin Oaks didn't set out to be one of the most ecologically sound communities in the US, it "just happened" because they followed the path of least resistance that income sharing opened up for them.)

So let's talk about how things are set up in income sharing groups. You can think of it kind of like a big family with shared finances. All income goes into one bank account and people's needs are met from that account. It can be structured in many different ways. Larger groups (like Twin Oaks and East Wind) tend to be more structured with some kind of formal labor management system and significant budget work happening each year. Smaller groups are often more casual, a lot more akin in structure to a family that just talks about things when new expenses come up — they usually have someone who keeps track of accounts and deals with tax filings, but they may or may not even track labor in any formal way.

Income sharing is almost always paired with collective ownership of housing, and this is another big plus for community. Collectively owning housing[72] opens the door for maximum community control over membership. Essentially housing comes with membership, and people do not have to arrive with enough money to be able to buy or build a home. If something turns out to really not be working and the community is faced with one of those awful decisions about asking someone to leave, you don't have the complications of them needing to sell a house in order to leave (and potentially asserting their legal rights to sell it to whoever they want to at maximum profit, which is unlikely to produce a great new community member for you).

Collectively owned housing is also a great setup for full life cycle community where someone can be born in the community, grow up there, pass through young adulthood, have their own kids (or not), be an empty nester and die in the community. If your housing needs can change over time and you don't have to go through a sale or a lease negotiation each time that happens, it's far less likely that those changed housing needs will result in you having to leave your community.

In the early days of Solidarity Collective, I moved multiple times within the collective in a short period of time as first my relationship shifted, then Covid 19 hit and I needed to quarantine, and finally other people needed the space I'd been living in more than I did. And it was not a big deal. I wasn't moving a kitchen because we had a communal kitchen in the main cooperative kitchen, and I had a bunch of folks around me willing to help carry boxes and furniture across the courtyard over a few days for some of the lowest stress moves I've ever experienced. Because *we* owned the housing instead of *me* owning it, it was also not a big deal emotionally or logistically to give up one space and move to another for the greater good.

There are also strong savings potential to income sharing. Say you have a membership that is currently collectively earning and spending $1M in an average year. By pooling together your resources and consumption, you may only need $750K to get everyone's needs met. Those savings come not just through being able to buy food in bulk and reducing the number of cars you collectively need, but also through substituting labor for money in activities like growing food and collective childcare.

---

72   To be clear, you can have an independent finances set up and still have housing owned collectively. It is a bit more complicated, but you can do it.

Finally, income sharing might not be as weird as you think it is: according to the Communities Directory, it's the way about 13% of established communities are set up now, and the last time I ran the numbers, the way about 18% of forming communities were intending to be set up. My speculation based on having my ear to the ground in the movement is that interest in this model will continue growing as the global economy continues to come apart at the seams.

So why am I spending so much ink on this topic? Am I saying income sharing is "the" right answer for communities? No. In some cases, it clearly is not. But you already know what a world structured around every family or individual for themselves is like to live in. I don't have to tell you what that looks and feels like. My hope is that in sharing more about this off-the-beaten-path option, you will give it some real consideration.[73]

Finances and Budgeting Basics

Once you have made the core decisions that affect your finances (income sharing or not, collectively or privately owned housing, whether you will have businesses collectively or not) you can start to put together a budget that reflects those decisions.

All communities will need a budget for:

- Property acquisition and maintenance, including taxes
- Future developments and long-term planning projects
- Legal fees and filings

Most communities will need a budget for:

- Common buildings and spaces
- Developing housing and its maintenance
- Social needs and committee expenses
- Training and consulting
- Whatever degree of land development is needed (which may include things like agricultural projects, roads, and utilities)
- potentially housing if it is collectively owned

Income sharing groups will additionally need a budget for:

- Collectively owned housing
- Living expenses including food, shelter, health insurance, and transportation

---

73   For more on this, see Matt Stannard's article about income sharing, here:
      https://truthout.org/articles/capitalism-killing-you-income-sharing-could-save-our-lives/.

- Budgets for shared businesses, and how they feed into the general community budget

The simple budget templates I've developed can be found at http://www.ic.org/building-belonging-resources. These can help you start to get concrete about how to create your budget.

Planning for Community Businesses

Building on the earlier discussion of aspects of business planning, I'd like to add a few more questions for your consideration around collective businesses.

How does this business align with your community mission? It can be fine for this answer to just be "it provides income to support the community or members of the community." What it should *not* do, however, is contradict your community values or mission. And folks are likely to be more excited to work in the community business if it does have a deeper alignment than just a paycheck. One of the real benefits of living in some types of community is being able to experience everything in your life moving in the same direction at the values level — a rare experience these days. Deeply aligned businesses can play a role in giving your members that experience.

Does it need its own legal entity? If it does, do the two entities have a formal relationship? Some business activities will make sense to fold into the community legal structure. For instance, if you decide to become an educational nonprofit, doing education programs is a good fit and would not need a separate entity. However, if you are an educational nonprofit and have a light manufacturing operation on the property, it probably needs a separate legal structure. The business might pay rent to the nonprofit, donate a percentage of their proceeds to the nonprofit, or simply provide jobs for members to be able to pay their community fees. Be clear about both the structures that hold different activities and what their relationship is and formalize that relationship in both a contract and an organizational structure chart.

Do you have a viable business plan? Regardless of how each entity is held legally, each needs its own business plan. This is very standard work of figuring out if this is a viable business. Questions include:

- What is the product or service and who are you marketing it to?
- Have you done competitor research and know there's a market for it that isn't already fully served?
- How much can you charge, and does that give you enough to meet the costs and provide good pay for workers (at a minimum) and profits if they are needed to contribute to the community?

How do you think about and value community labor that goes into the business? This is another instance where shared businesses within income sharing is the simpler option. If you are not income and labor sharing, then are you creating a partnership? Of all members? Only some? What if you need more labor temporarily? Will community members get first dibs on that work before you hire outside labor? How do basic "human resources" functions like hiring, firing, setting wages, and evaluations happen among community members?

How does this business relate to your community budget? It's essential to understand if this business is feeding money into the formal community budget in some way (tithing, profits being shared, leasing space from the community, etc), sharing any assets with the community that it holds joint responsibility for (a shared tractor or office space, for instance) or if it is a completely distinct entity financially. You can set it up a lot of ways, so just make sure you have a clear plan the group is on board with before launching it.

If it isn't a viable business, but you still want to do it, how does this fit with your mission, and how do you think about labor, time, and resources spent in the activity? You're going to be pretty busy in your forming years. Can your community budget swallow this enterprise without getting swamped? Take, for example, agricultural activities. Mainstream agriculture in the US relies on fairly abusive labor practices, and farm workers are paid very little for their time. You may not be able to compete as an outward facing business. However, farm work is also love work for a lot of people, and being able to farm as part of your contribution to the community can be a big quality of life booster for many people. The economic benefit to the community may be reduction of cash expenses in this case. Again, this is an area that you just want to talk and think through.

Exercise 14: Budgeting for Community Development

Spend some time fleshing out your development costs using a spreadsheet you create from scratch or my starter spreadsheet template. Do a little research on land prices in the place(s) you are considering, think about reasonable monthly obligations for the kind of community you want to create, research how much it costs to build like you want to build.

I ask everyone in my workshops on starting a community to spend at least 30 minutes looking at the spreadsheets, regardless of whether they will be playing a financial planning role in the community. That is really hard for some people who don't think of themselves as "numbers people" or find spreadsheets intimidating. (I was once one of those folks, and I still remember the anxiety it induced in me, so I am sympathetic!) I encourage this, however, because this is work that is deeply enough connected to so many other parts of the community development that everyone needs to have at least a rudimentary understanding of what the budget looks like in order to be able to help with decision-making. So please spend those 30 minutes at least and start to break the ice!

Labor Budgets

The last topic in this chapter is labor budgets. Money and labor are the two most concrete inputs that keep a community going. They are not more important than the social inputs, but they are both really important. Just like you need to have enough money flowing through the community to keep roofs over your heads, you also need to have enough labor happening to keep that roof in good repair.

Most communities, regardless of their economic structure, have at least some notion of what their labor needs are. Some groups uncover this gradually through a series of frustrated (and often projection-filled) conversations about what is not getting done. Others take a more proactive approach early on and do their best to anticipate what kinds of labor they will need.

Groups are all over the map about how they handle getting work done. Some have required hours per week, month, or year, and I've seen everything from 20 hours a year to 55 hours a week. Some rely solely on voluntary action, and some quantify participation in ways that aren't tied to hours (such as everyone needing to serve on at least one committee). Still others track labor very formally with spreadsheets and reporting systems.

My recommendation is to go through a process of needs assessment, budgeting, and contribution capacity around work, similarly to how you have done it with money. Here's some guidance on what to include in that conversation.

Track or trust?

Are we tracking hours in some way, or doing this on a trust-and-talk basis?

If tracking, what's the system for that? (Online, paper, etc.)

If tracking, are we tracking some general categories in order to have a sense of our labor needs over time?

If tracking, who has access to labor records? Everyone or just the labor accountant?

Both of these approaches can work, and they have upsides and downsides. On the one hand, tracking gives you a much more clear picture of what your labor needs actually are, makes your data geeks happy, and if done well, can help make otherwise invisible contributions visible. On the other hand, you need someone in charge of the tracking system and tracking requires its own investment of labor. And personal preferences and what motivates are almost always on a wide spectrum. Some people show up better when they feel like they are trusted to self-regulate. Others appreciate the clear expectations and self-check that a tracking system offers. If the group is on the fence about what to do, my advice is: try something. Give it six months with one answer and then talk about how it is going.

What counts?

It's a good idea to get clear about what things count, especially if you are tracking. General common categories:

- domestic tasks in common areas (including cooking for community, cleaning, organizing, etc.)
- construction, building, and grounds and equipment maintenance
- meetings, committee work, policy development, community trainings, mediation and other group process stuff
- correspondence and other tasks related to community member recruitment and retention
- labor system and financial accounting and planning
- "town trips" that collectivize shopping and driving labor
- events planning and hosting
- fundraising, including crowd funding and grant writing
- mission-aligned activism and volunteering in the wider community (usually limited hours)
- money-making work in a community business
- managing any systems the community relies on

For income sharing groups, I'd also consider adding:

- sick time
- pregnancy, birth, and recovery
- childcare and homeschooling
- agricultural work
- car maintenance

Notice that these lists are not all physical or all mental work, and they can tap into and value a lot of different skills. Once you have an initial list, you should also create a process for folks asking for something to be added.

How many hours?

Regardless of tracking or not, you will probably want some standard for hours of contribution. Again, this can vary widely depending on the nature of the community. Income sharing communities I know have done between 40 and 52 hours per week, depending largely on how comprehensive the list is of what counts and whether folks can bank hours toward vacation time or not. Non-income sharing groups vary between 20 hours per year and 10 hours per week. Some communities vary hours requirements based on the time of the year, and some have a subset of income producing work that is also on a quota.

This is another area where I'd suggest experimenting and evaluating.

Exceptions and exemptions?

The most common exceptions and reductions in requirements are for age, disability, pregnancy, and early parenting. You can also offer someone temporary reprieve during major life changes (you get two months off when you start a new high stress job for instance) or for bereavement. Having a wide range of what counts (specifically, not just physical labor) can help everyone feel included and valued by the system. The key here is to create a system that works for people in a diversity of circumstances, that is humane, and also is robust enough to get the work done.

I also want to name something that is developing quickly enough that I have not had time to figure out patterns in how to incorporate it well; consider this an invitation to be part of figuring it out together. Let's work to find ways to recognize and value emotional labor, either in this section or in the "What counts?" conversation. Some people (most often people in marginalized groups, especially women and BIPOC folks) are expected to do a lot of caretaking of others emotional needs, and to keep the peace by doing a lot of emotional gymnastics when oppression topics are brought up, and do a lot of free labor educating people about their own oppression. In progressive communities, it is worth having a conversation about how emotional labor intersects with your labor system.

Banking and gifting? (If tracking)

Do you let people take time off if they put in more than the required hours? In other words, can you "bank" hours? If someone is between jobs and has a lot of free time for a month, is it OK for them to do a lot and then take the rest of the year off? In income sharing groups that use tracking, this is a common mechanism for people to earn vacation time.

There is also an interesting question of whether someone with a positive balance can gift hours to someone else. Sometimes this in essence lets partners spell each other, and then the management of their labor becomes a joint responsibility. But you can also let anyone gift hours to anyone, opening the possibility of people supporting each other's self-care in that way, or just giving a gift because they want to.

Is there stuff everyone needs to do?

Cleaning up from common meals and participating in land-based work parties are the two most common things that groups put into this category. While being mindful of disability issues,[74] there are some definite benefits to having everyone show up in the basic physical labor of community (cleaning, cooking, painting buildings, pulling weeds, etc.). Many groups default into replicating the mainstream culture's value assessment of different kinds of work (paying more or giving more labor credits for "professional work" and expecting things like childcare to be volunteer hours, for instance) and you want to be mindful about the impact your valuation system will have on people living in the community.

Teenager hours requirement?

Some groups start labor requirements before the age of 18. There are definite pluses and minuses to this, including considering who if anyone gets to be the enforcer. But it is something else to consider.

Do you let people substitute money for labor?

This is a common practice, and one that can be very problematic from a diversity (and particularly class) perspective. If folks want to substitute, I'd encourage the group to ask why. If they are temporarily disabled (a broken leg, or long recovery from surgery) that's one thing. If they are a wealthy member who rarely participates in community life despite having significant leisure time, that's a very different thing, and letting someone

---

74   And here I mean not just physical disabilities but also neurodivergence and how that might impact someone's ability to "perform" at normie levels. Talking about contribution with everyone and not making assumptions can open the door to understand all the ways that neurodivergent and physically disabled people have a lot to offer that might not look like the standard "work" menu.

buy their way out of being an active community member will breed resentments more often than not.

Most people who are poor or working class (disproportionately people of color and single parents, especially single mothers) have limited time *and* money to contribute. Income and labor sharing is a systemic fix for this. But when you are not income sharing, you will have to grapple with how to be accessible for people with fewer financial resources *and* income, as well as less leisure time. Consider crafting *requirements* around the capacity of those who are most stretched thin, while creating a culture that encourages volunteering more time from those who can.

Exercise 15: Design a Labor System

Make significant agenda time for working through the labor system questions listed above. (Note you will not be able to do this work effectively without first answering, at a minimum, whether you are income sharing or independent finances.) Once you have answers to the questions settled, it is time to take a global look at your combined money and labor budgets and think about whether the overall contributions you are expecting from people are doable and reasonable. This is one of those moments where you may find yourself needing to either scale back your asks or scale up the number of people you think you need to have the project be viable.

CHAPTER 10: LEGAL STRUCTURES

Unless you're planning on just squatting (illegally occupying) some place to make your community home (and really, even if you are), or simply moving in together in a rented space, you're going to have to deal with laws and the legal profession when creating, living in, and shaping your community. And if and when your community folds, ends, disbands, or becomes a different community, more legal questions will come up. This chapter won't deal with all or even most of those legal questions, but it will help you think about the legal aspects of starting your community, and introduce you to places you can go to learn more or to obtain assistance with legal matters.

Every society and culture has rules around property, shared space, and how to "own" property, and every culture has its predominant values around the balances of rights and responsibilities of ownership. The United States, of course, leans strongly toward individual rights and individual property ownership in its values biases.

Our legal and economic systems reinforce a cultural orientation around powerful individuals buying and selling things, with ordinary folks expected to model those captains of industry by saving for a house, taking on mortgages, maybe doing some small-scale buying, selling, and renting of property.

This often supercharged individualistic, competitive energy, among other things, can make a new community's search for a legal structure deeply dissatisfying to the kinds of people who want to build intentional communities. The worlds of law, finance, and real estate are where we most directly have to grapple with American individualism. I so often hear community-builders, when talking about legal entities and financial choices, say things like "Nothing fits. Nothing feels good." And that's because, at least in most parts of the country, the law **doesn't** really recognize or understand community.

But there's a bright side to this: There are resources, smart and hard-working innovators and change-makers, heroic organizations, creative lawyers, real estate-experts, researchers and community-builders who are helping create alternative views of law and property — and they want you to talk to them! At certain points in the chapter I will name particular resources, groups, and individuals who can help with certain things. In networking with and learning from these individuals and groups, you can not only work on solutions that fit your community's needs, but also be part of the collective effort to create new legal realities.

Let's start with this premise for our challenge: ***The more radically a community wants to organize its land and economic systems, the more legally challenging it becomes.***

Here's a high level summary of some of those frustrations.

1. Many laws and available legal structures for your community may be based on different values than your own. Laws around ownership either assume you want to make a lot of money, or make it hard for you to make any money at all. Many options might be available but feel uncomfortable.

2. Laws about organizations and property are ableist and classist. The easiest and one of the most universally available legal structures, the Limited Liability Company or LLC, can make it difficult or impossible to receive Social Security Disability Insurance (commonly referred to simply as "Disability") or enroll in a health insurance plan through the Affordable Care Act.[75] The very fact that you need financial and social capital to purchase property is prohibitive to most Americans.

3. Available legal structures and applicable laws are inconsistent. Worker-owned cooperatives and Permanent Real Estate Cooperatives (PRECs) are closer in intent to collective management, but are not an option in every state and might not be a good fit in other ways.

4. Available legal structures are difficult to navigate. Community land trusts (CLTs) and the apostolic association (common purse) 501(d) structure were both designed to support community living, but are hard to set up and come with restrictions.[76]

5. Competent professional support can be hard to find. On top of the overwhelming amount of information and choices you have to process through to make legal decisions, very few lawyers, financers, real estate agents, and accountants know anything about intentional communities. A lot of the time, they aren't much help and you spend money educating them.

6. State and municipal laws are often against you. You'll run into restrictions on ecological tech, limits to how many unrelated people can live under one roof,[77] etc., which are built into zoning laws and local ordinances in some places.

---

75   This is because there are caps on how much money you can make on Disability, and in states that did not expand Medicaid to cover low income people, the ACA also has both a maximum and a *minimum* amount you need to make. Not being able to predict if the gains and losses from the business will keep someone within that sweet spot of government eligibility can mean that folks who need Disability or the ACA to survive may not be willing to risk those benefits by joining your community.

76   Some groups combine multiple structures in order to derive the benefits of both structures, but that gets complicated fast. One option is to have a land trust hold the property and function as the property developer and manager, then have an educational nonprofit which runs the community and does education and outreach work that benefits the wider world.

77   For years I've thought those laws were just a relic of the past, but recently a new one was passed in Florida with an 8-0 vote by the council. Structural barriers to communal living are alive and well.

A brief cautionary tale, from an actual person.

I wanted to share a back and forth I recently had with someone who had taken one of my online courses. It is not unusual for me to get this kind of message, but this one did such a good job of summing up the challenges, I got permission to share a lightly edited (for anonymity) version of their message and my response.

Hi Yana,

I took a course from you last year from the IC.org website on starting a community. I had done EXACTLY what you said NOT to do and just bought a large duplex mid-2020 and started filling it with people to start a community.

While I had the best of intentions and have tried to be transparent and aware about the challenge of power dynamics in the house, I have had the following issues.

1. You were right. As the 48 year old owner of the property, I am pretty much mom and landlord. People come to me if they need a tool or something fixed, or an improvement done. And to babysit their dogs, provide lightbulbs, kill spiders in their rooms, clean toilets and carpets before new people move in, and manage all the vendors of the house. Since I work from home, it's always me. Mom, maid, housekeeper, and landlord.

2. When someone moves out, we have agreed to use consensus on choosing new housemates. Everyone pays a fixed rent on their rooms. Since I carry the cost and people like the extra space and silence of a whole side of the house to themselves, no one is in any rush to find a new housemate except for me. We've had 2 rooms empty for 3 months. Another empty for 6 months. The process has been highly influenced by a woman who says she's looking for someone who's self-aware and is a hard pass after a 30 minute talk with most prospective roommates — especially if they are a person of color, from a different culture, or have kids.

3. My housemates/community have talked about wanting to help out and get involved but essentially I have to hire out most landscaping/garden/maintenance work. If I want something done within 3 months, I need to do it myself. I can't do much of it myself because I have a very full time job and a chronic illness. But for example, I bought a large table for the other side of the duplex so they could host house dinners comfortably. I have provided a truck they can use any time — it comes in easy to manage pieces and just ask that

they pick it up themselves from the store. We are still waiting for that errand 3 months later.

4. I thought if people were co-owners in the property that there might be more buy-in from tenants but I have not found a way to really co-own the property since banks will not make a loan to a tenant to own a portion of a duplex. I could do a TIC[78] with the other side of the duplex but I've had problems finding a whole family who wants to live in community. It's been easier to fill rooms although easy is not what I would call it at this point.

On top of this, I run a very full time business, am a single parent of a tween, and suffer from chronic fatigue that makes handling the additional responsibilities of the house really tough.

I feel like I might have made a tremendous mistake. I am looking at a cohousing group in town that broke ground last year, but I'm not sure how I would even unwind what I've begun here. And I hate to uproot my daughter again. I don't want to make any quick decisions. But each day brings a new host of scenarios that feels like more evidence that, while I do get to live with people I really love, I have created another full time job for myself which feels like it will put me in an early grave or bankrupt me or both.

Another possibility is to build a tiny house on the property here and just rent out the duplex which would allow me to live on this beautiful property but I would miss the community aspect if I had to just rent out to muggles not interested in community. It's just all a mixed bag. No gain without a loss and vice versa.

Any advice or resources that you would suggest? I feel like such an idiot. And I'm sure that I've done this to myself. But I'm not sure what the next steps could or should even be.

I so appreciate it! Thanks so much!

Sad Sole Owner

Hey Sad,

My heart aches reading this. This isn't surprising to me, but I hate seeing real people get caught up in this kind of thing.

---

[78] Tenants In Common.

I think it is hard to transition away from an initial set up like this. People are often more drawn to what is than what you are hoping it will become, and right now people have a pretty sweet setup with you doing a lot higher % of the hard stuff and taking on all of the risk. Where to go from here . . . I can't really tell you what you should do, but there are some possibilities that occur to me.

I know of a few groups who have gotten off the ground by moving in together for a set period of time in order to both save some money and learn some initial skills for living together and making decisions together. If you can find folks who you think would be a good core group with you, one possibility is to say, "Hey, I've got space that we can use for a few years while we get our vision and social structures together." If you did that, I'd ask people to assume the risk along with you, meaning you split the actual costs equitably. Maybe some of the folks there already would fit that bill . . .?

You can also become a great landlord. I know this isn't what you want, but whether you do the tiny house thing or join that new cohousing community or stay put and screen people based on your own standards, it may make sense at this point to re-assume the reins. If people are using the power they have with consensus to stop the project from being economically viable and letting the full burden of it sit in your lap, that's an abuse of the process. The rights of consensus need to be appropriately paired with responsibility for the impacts (and work) that decisions create. Sounds like there is a mismatch currently.

You can also call this a lesson learned and start over. (Again, this sucks as you have already invested a lot of time and money and your daughter needs stability.) If folks in the community want to get together and figure out how to buy the property from you, they could do that. But like I said, trying to reboot from the place where you are and have it be more communally-held and managed and held is really uphill.

If you do decide to stick it out on this property and try to convert to more of an egalitarian community, it may make sense to look for non-traditional funding (like loans from people you know, who would not have the same restrictions as a bank).

I'm not sure any of this will be things you have not already thought of or if there is something new here. What I can definitely validate for you though is that this is a hard and not uncommon thing.

I hope this helps! Yana

So I get why so many of us avoid the legal questions for as long as we can. This avoidance also sometimes leads to those who own property already deciding to take the "easy" way out and just retain ownership of the property and invite others to join them to "make a community." The sidebar will give you an insider's peek into my email and one person's experience with why this can have unintended and really damaging consequences. I strongly caution against structures that maintain individual ownership of property meant for the entire community. But if I'm going to advise you not to do something, I need to show you the options that do exist.

Finding the right legal structure is about creating checks and balances on the power of ownership, and making sure everyone is protected as much as possible from financial and legal risks. While the struggles of the owner described in the sidebar are serious and painful, the risks to the non-owning residents in the same scenario are also extremely serious. The owner has the ability to pull the rug out from under the rest of the group, and the full backing of the legal system to do it. Even if you would never do that (or think you never would) it is very hard for people to fully relax and invest themselves energetically in the project when this is a possibility.

In order to head that off, I strongly recommend you navigate this sticky territory, have property held by some collective entity (at least a simple LLC), and have the whole group, or as many of them as legally possible, assume the responsibility for being owners together.

When you are transitioning a property from sole to collective ownership, clear and carefully made agreements are critical. You should all sit down and talk about, and then lay out, how and when the property will be placed into collective ownership. This may include preconditions for each step, such as X number of people living on the property for at least one year. It should also include how the sale price will be determined (if selling it is how you are transferring ownership).

Thus far, we've assumed the kinds of community property people are trying to find are presumably buildings and land that can basically be occupied together. But some communities, like Dancing Rabbit Ecovillage in Missouri, hold the land in common while letting folks make, sell, and buy homes on the land.

Let's return to a topic that we talked around a bit in Chapter 9's "big economic questions": Should individuals or the community as a whole own the housing? Here's a short pros and cons list for both possibilities.

Pros of private ownership of housing:

1. It's familiar. People understand it, it seems safe, professionals can support it easily, and there are common legal structures that work.

2. You will be able to dodge some of the harder conversations about money and personal rights. You will still need to talk about equity and inheritance issues, but the list of hard conversations is shorter.

3. It's easier to purchase and pay for. Depending on your local lending scene, it will probably be easier for folks to get individual mortgages than trying to get a loan for a project that local financiers may not understand. And if you need to work with banks, they will be much more likely to lend to you.[79]

Cons of private ownership of housing:

1. People may get stuck in non-consensual relationship with the community (unable to sell their home) or become absentee landlords, which can be really bad for everyone. This happens when a community requires that people become members before they can buy a house. This leads to a really small buyers market, and I know people who have had houses for sale for a decade in a community they moved on from in every other way years earlier.

2. Alternatively, the community can also lose control of its own membership process. If, instead of requiring membership, people can sell their houses directly to just anyone (who would presumably become members after they buy the house), you will lose control over membership selection. I've seen lots of cases where a disgruntled member, upon leaving, listed their home on the open market and the people moving in had no idea they were moving into a community. Mission drift is almost inevitable in cases like these.

3. Financial profit is a problematic motivation for community, and private ownership often comes with the promise of being able to build wealth through homeownership. If you aren't going to let people build equity, you need to be very clear about that at the beginning. And if you are, you need to be willing to live with the consequences of profit motive competing with your vision for people's loyalties and attention.

---

79   They may, however, view this as a business loan, which can mean it will have a higher interest rate than home loans.

Pros of collective ownership of housing:

1. People can move much more easily between housing as their needs change without dealing with sales and legal transfers. This significantly increases the likelihood that people will be able to stay in the community as their needs change, which can get you that vital longevity of membership. Because people do not have to deal with selling and buying a home in order to change the type of housing they live in, these models accommodate more of the full life cycle for a lot of people. For many of us, this is an ideal of deep long term relationships that motivates a move to community.

2. Collective ownership best protects the community's ability to choose members. If access to housing comes with membership, rather than the other way around, you can feel free to vet new members within legal bounds (see sidebar on page 155 for more on Fair Housing Law). You can also give people the opportunity to come live with you for a limited time while you are all getting to know each other. If someone has to buy a house to get that experience, it makes it much harder for everyone to walk away if it isn't working.

3. Collective ownership is generally more compatible with economic justice as it socializes the costs of buying and maintaining housing and lets the group decide how they want to relate to space, money, and needs around housing.

4. Collective ownership eliminates the often predatory and always power-laden landlord-tenant relationships within the community. The community can create even-handed ways of deciding how space is distributed, and hold each other accountable to those processes.

Cons of collective ownership of housing

1. Conversations about money, equity, and inheritance rights are hard. Not only will you have to have deeper versions of each of these conversations, but explaining to incoming members that they don't have the ability to build equity (or that it is limited) or pass housing down to their heirs will almost certainly lose you a few otherwise interesting potential members.

2. Collective ownership complicates the ways property can create equity. The standard model of equity-building is tied to the market and requires being able to sell the property at some point. But if you aren't able to sell, equity is going to have to be more challenging to distribute.[80]

---

80   For instance, one founder I'm in conversation with is considering a model where the community owns all of the buildings and there is a monthly fee for living on the property with a small added amount that would go into a savings account. When someone leaves, they would be given back that extra money they put in along with any interest their contributions earned.

3. Again: legal, financial, and real estate pros often don't understand it.

4. Collective ownership is a paradigm shift for those who live it. Membership recruitment may be harder; values alignment needs to be stronger. (This is obviously a pro as well as a con if it works out, but generally it means slower growth and some groups need a lot of people early on to get onto property.)

What about rentals?

Some communities don't have any rental options at all. Income sharing communities, for instance, usually have housing come with membership. There are other types of communities as well where all of the housing is collectively owned (owned by the same legal entity as the commons areas). In these cases, there tends to be significant flexibility to people getting their housing needs met.

Communities that are still invested in a private ownership model for housing can still get some of these benefits by making rentals an option. Renting is generally more accessible for people of less economic means who may not have the credit ratings and savings to get a traditional loan (or family and friend connections to wealth), and changing rentals is a lot easier than selling and buying a house — even if the timing magically works out that the kind of unit you now need comes available very closely in time to when you are selling your current unit.

Some cautionary notes on rental dynamics in community:

Never make it so renters have less decision-making power than owners simply by virtue of being renters/owners. Don't make ownership a criteria for decision-making. This (unfortunately common) practice reinforces classist dynamics of the wider culture (where money equals power) which also tends to affect women's, BIPOC, and trans folks' access to power in the community since we are disproportionately less wealthy. It also removes a portion of the creative energies and skills your community can draw on by cutting some folks out.

It can also undermine people's dedication to the community. Although I've seen exceptions where renters have made long term commitments to the community in spite of being locked out of decision-making, they have been just that: exceptions. Most of the time when we're locked into legal and economic hierarchies, we tend to behave in ways heavily influenced by those positions.

The arguments for not including renters in at least some forms of decision-making (anything dealing with the property and collectively owned buildings for instance) tend to fall into two categories: the circular or the oppressive. The circular argument is that renters aren't fully committed or don't have a vested interest in good decisions about the property, which becomes a self-fulfilling prophecy. The oppressive argument is that renters won't care about property values. This one may actually be correct, but I strongly encourage you to consider whether that is something we **ought** to be protecting given the unhealthy power dynamic and model of community it creates.

Even if you've made an effort to flatten the power differentials between renters and owners, there are still interpersonal challenges to renting within community. Whoever the owner of the unit is (either private individuals within the community who own more than one unit and rent some of them out to other members, or the community as a whole) has significant power over the people renting from them just by virtue of owning.

When you rent in community, someone else ultimately gets to decide if you get to stay, and your only option if you want to stay and they want you to leave is to participate in an adversarial legal relationship with them. Individual states and municipalities vary widely in the balance of rights between landlords and tenants, but whether an angry landlord has the power to render a tenant suddenly homeless, or an angry tenant has the power to stay longer than the landlord wants, it's a recipe for festering anger and explosive conflict benefitting nobody.

Even if that power is never abused, it hangs in the space, and may make it harder for renters to be authentic about what they think and feel, particularly if it means disagreeing with their landlord, or friends of their landlord. I've seen multiple unfortunate situations where owners of units were asked by other community members to put pressure on their renters to toe the line on some issue or another. This is ugly, and the kind of dynamic that should have no place in community.

Some communities try to avoid the dynamics of the landlord-tenant relationship by "re-defining" owners and residents in more cooperative-sounding terms, trying to create a partnership between the owner and non-owner. These efforts are usually sincere and well-intended. The problem is that courts and cops will still recognize the relationship as landlord-tenant if that's what it looks like (the non-owner is paying the owner, the owner is providing the housing, each side with traditional rights and responsibilities).

Finally, if the community owns the rental units, maintaining those units makes for additional community labor that has to come from somewhere, and the last thing any community needs is more work to do. If, after reading all these cautionary notes your community still wants to make renting an option, you should carefully consider how you will face these challenges.

Understanding the basics of Fair Housing Law

by guest contributor Harvey Baker

Federal Fair Housing Law (FHL), passed in 1968, was designed to end the rampant housing discrimination common before its passage. It defines seven "protected classes" (categories of people) that it is illegal to discriminate against. It applies to anyone operating in the housing world (realtors, house owners, landlords, advertisers, advertising publishers, banks and other lending institutions, etc.).

The seven protected classes are race, color, religion, sex, national origin, family status, and (added in 1988) disability status. The law was written very broadly, and the few exceptions were written very narrowly (e.g., religious groups can discriminate in favor of people of the same religion as long as they don't discriminate against other protected classes.) States may not remove Federal protected classes, but may add their own (such as age, lawful source of income, marital status, sexual orientation, and more.) For information on state laws, see https://www.craigslist.org/about/state_fair_housing_laws#KN.

Generally, because residential intentional communities provide housing for people in one way or another, it is illegal for communities to discriminate against protected classes in choosing their members/residents. It is legal to discriminate on the basis of countless other characteristics (financial ability, diet, vaccination status, allergy to peanut butter, etc., etc.), just not the Federal protected classes or any your state has added. Community people often ask, "But can't I choose who I want to live with?" The answer is, "only within the constraints of Fair Housing Law."

One of the interesting and challenging aspects of FHL is that it was written to eliminate certain common discriminations, such as against people of color or families with children, but was written in a neutral way that also prohibits discrimination against people previously privileged in the housing market (for example, white people or couples without children).

For more information, see the HUD website: https://www.hud.gov/program_offices/fair_housing_equal_opp/fair_housing_act_overview.

Determining Your Legal Structure(s)

Once you are clear about the core ownership, membership, and economic models you want to follow, that will narrow the field of options that make sense for legal structures. In some ways, this whole book has been designed to get you to this chapter already having thought about the major criteria that will feed into your decision-making on legal structures.

Let's keep a couple of things in mind as we go through this part. First, here's where you'll feel some of the frustrations and challenges we listed at the very beginning of the chapter: laws and structures are very location-specific, there are often webs of building and zoning codes complicating your community dreams, and it's not always easy to get sound legal advice about how to do what you want to do. I've organized information about the most common factors groups weigh in deciding what structure to use into a chart, which is on page 166.

Second, regardless of what structure you choose, be aware that every community has to abide by Fair Housing Law, meaning you cannot discriminate (either for or against) on the basis of what is called a "protected class."[81] Additionally, your property may also be subject to Americans with Disabilities Act requirements, which can be challenging if you are purchasing older or non-ADA compliant property.

That said, here's some starter info to get your conversations rolling.

There are three legal structures that were designed with some form of community in mind: housing cooperatives, community land trusts, and apostolic associations. All three can be easily structured to act as a buffer against profit motive running your decision-making, and thus have the potential to be part of a strategy for affordable housing and lifestyles, and economic justice work. If your community vision and ownership desires can fit neatly into one of these and they are available where you are, then you will have less need for "hacking the system" (as my colleague Cassandra Ferrera calls it) to have the structure support your mission. Here's a brief introduction to each one, and some resources specific to their type of community.

Housing Cooperatives (AKA Mutual Benefit Corporation)

Cooperatives are usually structured so that you own a share of the co-op rather than the home itself. You can relate to equity building in a variety of ways with Market Rate

---

81   The federal Fair Housing Act and its 1988 amendments protect people from negative housing actions that occur because of their race, color, national origin, religion, sex, disability, or family status. States may add additional categories and that is one of the main reasons why you need to get familiar with your specific location's legal landscape. You can have membership processes like those described in Chapter 8, and mission documents as described in Chapter 5 that center certain people or life experiences, but you can't block anyone from being part of your community on the basis of one of these categories.

Co-ops, Limited Equity Co-ops, and Leasing Co-ops which are a non-equity building option. Individuals and families may be able to get what is called a "share loan" that functions a lot like a mortgage, and can take the same tax breaks as homeowners.

Like all legal forms, co-ops need to abide by Fair Housing Law and cannot discriminate based on protected classes. However, they can otherwise engage in mission-based membership sorting, and those standards are set by the owner-member group. Co-ops have been successfully used in many places, for instance, to provide long term affordable housing for artists in some very expensive and volatile housing markets.

Cooperatives are home to the largest number of communitarians in the US, getting a healthy boost from the many student co-ops around the country in university towns, and also being a structure of choice for a lot of affordable housing nonprofits.

There are a number of great resources[82] to help you think about cooperatives as a possible legal structure for your group, including the California Center for Cooperative Development, the Cooperative Development Institute, the NorthEast Investment Cooperative (which is actually in Minnesota) and the North American Students of Cooperation (NASCO, which contrary to its name does not just work with student co-ops) in addition to the aforementioned East Bay Permanent Real Estate Cooperative. NASCO also has a sister organization called NASCO Properties that owns and supports the running of co-op houses all over the country. Groups can connect with them if they want to explore being part of a network of co-ops.

Land Trusts

Land trusts come in two flavors — the Community Land Trust (which is designed to ensure permanently affordable housing) or the Conservation Land Trust (which is designed to protect the land from ecologically harmful development). Both kinds of land trusts remove land permanently from the speculative housing market, which can be a very good thing for long term stability. Both fall into the "nonprofit" family of structures for the IRS, and the donation of land and other real property to either kind of LT comes with significant tax benefits for the donor. And both versions get used sometimes for intentional communities.

Conservation LTs essentially create voluntary (though legally binding) restrictions on how the property can be developed. This can bring tax benefits with it because development potential is a large factor in property valuation for taxation purposes. It is also

---

82   http://www.cccd.coop/,
     https://cdi.coop/,
     http://www.neic.coop/,
     https://www.nasco.coop/.

a useful mechanism for materializing your community values around sustainability and resilience. For groups interested in going this route, the national Land Trust Alliance is an excellent resource.[83]

Community LTs make affordable housing a long term priority. Not all Community LTs are the kind of high-participation self-governed communities that most of us are seeking in wanting to create a community, but this is a well-matched legal form if that is your goal and economic justice is a priority. The Grounded Solutions Network is a good place to start if this sounds like a good match with your focus.[84] There are also just a lot of Community LTs in the US — roughly 225 at the time this book was published.

A smaller, more regional network of communities organized as LTs, the School of Living, founded in 1934 is the owning entity for six of those communities in Pennsylvania, Virginia, and Maryland.[85] SoL is a wealth of information and deep knowledge about community building and living.

Neither type of Land Trust necessarily dictates whether the community or individuals own all or some of the housing. Community Land Trusts generally have individual ownership of housing as the default however, so make sure you are paying attention to those details and including special provisions if you want to do collective ownership. Clifford Paulin suggests that, "a co-op or some other legal entity could just as easily hold the master lease from the CLT and then members could have their own legal relationship with that subservient (in the legal sense) entity."[86]

Land Trusts also allow for mixed use development (housing, businesses, agriculture, etc) making them a good match with many founder's intentions for a fully featured community, assuming you can find the zoning to allow this, or get an exemption for it. Finally, because they keep housing affordable over the long term, they can be used to combat gentrification, making sure that residents will not be priced out of communities they have a long term relationship with.

LTs can hold property for just one community (like Dancing Rabbit Ecovillage) or a whole network of communities, usually in a defined geographic area (like School of Living does). It is worth investigating if there is an LT in your area already that could serve as the holder of your property. If you did that, you would want a really clear contract with the LT, and will probably also still need a legal entity for organizing the other activities

---

83   https://www.landtrustalliance.org/land-trusts.

84   https://groundedsolutions.org/.

85   https://www.schoolofliving.org/ SOL's mission includes: "assisting individuals to become more responsible and self-reliant, nurturing healthy, Land Trust Communities, promoting ecological use of land and natural resources, empowering inquiry and action on local and global problems, and working to develop and implement approaches to a more just and free society."

86   Personal communication, May 26, 2022.

of the community. The Agrarian Trust is another good resource for folks exploring this model, as they have worked on bridging between Community and Conservation LTs.[87]

One precautionary note about LTs: As a member of the nonprofit family, LTs are going to legally require you to have a Board of Directors. I recommend that if you go this route, you be very clear about which body (the Board or the membership) is responsible for which types of decisions, and build those clear lines into your bylaws.

Apostolic Associations (the 501d)

The least well known legal structure that was designed with community in mind is probably the Apostolic Association. It was originally created by the Internal Revenue Service for the Shakers, and is closely associated in some people's minds with monasteries, ashrams, and other spiritual or religious communities. However, the IRS has a surprisingly open-minded interpretation of the code,[88] and simply having well-articulated values in common can fit the definition of "apostolic."

So where is the line? It is about having a "common purse." or income sharing. And since somewhere around 13% of the communities movement shares income, this one is probably of interest to a number of aspiring founders who have picked up this book.

Major assets (land, housing, farming, and businesses' infrastructure and equipment) are all owned by the community in this model. All[89] income that comes from community or individual sources goes into a collective pot, with the community providing for member needs from this same pot. So the core features of these communities are collective ownership, shared income and expenses, and shared values.

Income sharing has a lot of direct benefits, as I detailed In Chapter 9. Because money and assets are held in common, resource sharing is a no-brainer, and that is one of the biggest leverage points for reducing carbon footprints.[90] It is also possible to design labor sharing systems that embody gender and class equity, where one hour of labor is counted equally with any other, whether that work is "domestic" or income producing, white collar or blue collar. That flies directly in the face of the capitalism-fueled hierarchies that assign dignity and high worth based on unspoken standards that may have little to do with genuine necessity or societal value.[91]

---

87 https://www.agrariantrust.org/.

88 See the helpful IRS document found here: https://www.irs.gov/pub/irs-pdf/p5627.pdf.

89 Some 501d communities allow members to keep a small portion of personal income, so long as they are also fully meeting their obligations to the group, however they have that defined.

90 I document this in more detail in *Together Resilient: Building Community in the Age of Climate Disruption*, 2007.

91 Think about how we all became familiar with the terms "essential workers" during Covid, and how those roles typically make the lowest wages in the economy.

Social justice is not the only thing that can flow naturally from income sharing.[92] I mentioned in the chapter on economic structures that income sharing is one of the top three factors in long term satisfaction with community living. I suspect this is in part because of the economic security that comes with this form of community. All of that said, you have to be prepared to do some strong culture change to have this model work well (and that means a fair bit of personal growth work to support it). The redefinition of security away from that individualistic framework is good work, but big work.

In addition to that hard work, the model itself has some fairly annoying limitations imposed by IRS code. The community needs to be generating at least half of the income it relies on from collective activities on the property, and the most common interpretation of that is that you have to make at least 50% of your income from activities on the property. That means that if you are envisioning a model where your members only have outside jobs, you won't be able to use this model.

An LLC or one of the other business partner based legal structures may be a better choice for that scenario. However, if you are inclined to something like a retreat center, farming, or small scale manufacturing as your primary economic base, you may be able to meet the 50% test. Some of the best known US communities are ones you can look to for how this model can be leveraged, including Twin Oaks Community, East Wind Community, and Acorn Community. All three of these groups are member communities of the Federation of Egalitarian Communities[93] which requires member communities to be democratically controlled, thereby excluding many 501(d) communities with sole leaders.

---

92   To be clear, I'm highlighting the potential here. There are a lot of communities that use income sharing in ways that are definitely not what would be fairly called socially progressive.

93   https://www.thefec.org/.

More about the Federation of Egalitarian Communities

The FEC website includes profiles of their member communities, communities-in-dialogue (who meet most but not all of their values, or are working toward becoming members) and allied communities. It also has a page called "systems and structures" that is worth checking out if you are seriously considering going this route.

From the FEC website:

The FEC is a union of Egalitarian Communities which have joined together in our common struggle to create a lifestyle based on Equality, Cooperation, and Harmony with the Earth.

Our Principles

Each of the FEC communities:

- Holds its land, labor, income and other resources in common.
- Assumes responsibility for the needs of its members, receiving the products of their labor and distributing these and all other goods equally, or according to need.
- Practices non-violence.
- Uses a form of decision making in which members have an equal opportunity to participate, either through consensus, direct vote, or right of appeal or overrule.
- Actively works to establish the equality of all people and does not permit discrimination on the basis of race, class, creed, ethnic origin, age, sex, sexual orientation, or gender identity
- Acts to conserve natural resources for present and future generations while striving to continually improve ecological awareness and practice.
- Creates processes for group communication and participation and provides an environment which supports people's development.

Other viable and common structure options

Home Owners Association (HOA), Planned Unit Development, Condo Association

These are different names for essentially the same structure. HOA's have traditionally been the structure of choice for most cohousing-style communities. They are definitely easy to find competent professional support to set up, and banks are very familiar with them, making for one less headache in the financing department. HOAs are:

> "[D]esigned for individuals or households who have a deed to their own lot, house, apartment, or housing unit, and shared ownership of common property. These entities offer tax advantages — all funds collected from members and spent on buying, developing, managing, repairing, or maintaining the property are tax deductible."[94]

They have two significant downsides, though, and I've worked with many cohousing groups over the years who are really struggling with the fallout from this choice. The first is that it is trickier to do solid member selection than with any other structure. The second (which is not unique to HOAs, but for some reason seems to play out worse with this model) is that it requires a Board of Directors and groups often devolve into decision-making power struggles between the Board and community. If you are going to use this structure, I'd recommend having the legally required officers sit on committees appropriate to their role (such as having the Treasurer on the Finance Team) and basically making the "Board" the whole membership of the community, eliminating or significantly blunting this dual governance conflict.

This structure also reinforces the US individualism tendency more than most. They are, for instance, the only structure that *must* have private ownership of the housing (though most others have this option). So if collective ownership seems like a better match for your group, you'll want to pass on this option.

There is also an interesting finance quirk with HOAs — the 60% rule: at least 60% of the community's income needs to come from dues, fees and assessments for maintaining and managing infrastructure. That means that it makes collective business endeavors more difficult, needing a separate legal structure to do that if it will pass the 40% mark, including things like renting the common house out for events or office space to members, or a community agriculture business on the property.

Finally, for practical (and in some places, legal) reasons, HOAs are set up so that home sales are market rate, with full equity-building potential. While some other structures also allow for that, no other structure has that as a fundamental feature.

Limited Liability Company (LLC)

LLCs are not only a viable model for the long run, they are also fast and easy to set up and therefore serve sometimes as a "starter structure" for groups. As the name implies, LLCs have the advantage of providing some legal protection for individuals who are part of the community. While the community or individuals within the community may get sued for something the community has done, individuals are essentially protected

---

from at least having their assets seized. Members are business partners, and each member has shares in the company. Taxes are handled with the LLC serving as a pass-through entity — members have a percentage of any profits or losses that are claimed on their personal taxes.

I mentioned in the introduction to this chapter the limits of LLCs in real time and space for people on Disability and using the Affordable Care Act in states that did not expand Medicaid. This creates a significant problem for groups with social justice values and trying to be economically accessible.

On the other hand, because you are business partners, there is a solid mechanism for being able to do member selection within the confines of Fair Housing Law, and there are no issues with dual Board-member governance like with HOAs and the nonprofit family of structures. One possible downside is that banks often view LLC property ownership as an investment property and may therefore charge you higher interest rates like a business.

This structure is also one of the few on this list that is universally available in all 50 states.

Nonprofits

Also available in all 50 states is becoming a nonprofit. (Technically, both Apostolic and Land Trust groups I've mentioned earlier are part of this family, but in this case I mean a more well-known educational nonprofit, a 501c3.) For groups with a strong educational or service orientation, it might be worth wading through the significant paperwork and hoops needed to become a nonprofit. You would also reap the core benefit that nonprofits of all kinds do, being able to take tax deductible donations to support your mission.

Since nonprofits are able to own real property, this model is flexible in terms of being able to do individually owned homes on leased land the nonprofit owns, and having housing and land owned by the nonprofit. Clifford Paulin adds this caveat if the community owns the housing that people are leasing: "It should be noted that if a individual or family is going to own the home and lease from the nonprofit, there will have to be a demonstration that the rate paid is fair market value lest the nonprofit run afoul of the 'private inurement' rule and jeopardize the tax exempt status of the nonprofit."[95]

Nonprofit law is fairly complex, and it will be important to work with an attorney who understands how to mesh this structure with a community.

---

95   Personal communication, May 26, 2022.

Any of the nonprofit options are going to require a Board of Directors as part of your governance structure, and (unlike HOAs which expect Board members to live in the community) at least 50% of that Board needs to be disinterested or non-benefiting people, meaning in most interpretations that they can't live in the community. If you have big mission ambitions, this can be fine and even really helpful to keep you on track and have fresh perspective regularly infusing some aspects of the project. However, you want to be really clear about domains of power and responsibility within decision-making so that people who are not well enough informed about daily life in the community are not being able to make decisions that are below the mission-level. How the kitchen gets cleaned, for instance, needs to be decided by residents, not the Board.

Tenancy in Common (TIC) and Joint Tenancy (JT)

Like LLCs, both of these models are very easy to set up. In some places, one of these models may be what the state considers the default (usually for couples, but communities can get lumped into this as well, barring having another structure in place).

With a TIC, multiple names will be listed on the property title. JTs can be set up by adding language to the deed, with no additional paperwork needing to be filed. One drawback to both of these structures is that people can sell their property to anyone without a membership process so that the remaining members have a say in who they live with. Members share equally in the benefits and liabilities of the community, but may find themselves dealing with a lawsuit or being forced into selling the property by a departing member or in cases of bankruptcy of a member. If you use one of these structures, I strongly recommend building additional structure and restrictions to protect the integrity of the community, including severability clauses to protect against being pulled into an individual's financial challenges.

While I know some communities (especially small ones) go this route, I'd be cautious about choosing this as the drawbacks can be very impactful on the group.

Inheritance issues

One last essential question related to legal rights is what someone's heirs can inherit. There are three possible answers to that: property (usually a house), the value of the property, and membership in the community. You will definitely want to consult with a lawyer on this question and make sure you are protecting the community membership selection process in a way that is legally compatible with the legal structure you choose.

I strongly recommend never letting heirs inherit membership. If someone is a good fit for the community, then they should be able to go through the same process their parent(s) did in order to join. If they aren't then you need a mechanism for them to be able to recover the value of the property they have inherited, and it is definitely best to spell that out as part of your core economic structure documents.

See the Figure 9: Legal Structures Chart for some barebones information about this topic.

Summing up key considerations in choosing a legal structure:

- Can own property in the best way to support your vision
- Are able to select members to the degree appropriate for your project
- It supports your priorities around equity and inheritance issues
- Have a clear entry and exit processes that you have run past a lawyer
- Is available where you want to be
- Ease of changes to bylaws and members
- Community is legally protected from bad actors

The following chart is designed to help you organize your collective thoughts on the subject of choosing a legal structure. While there are a lot of nuances a chart like this can't capture, it's a solid place to start, and is probably most helpful as a tool to narrow your choices down in preparation for talking to a local lawyer.

TRAITS OF LEGAL STRUCTURES

	Privately Owned Housing Allowed	Collectively Owned Housing Allowed	Board required?	Can you control membership?
Tenancy in Common	Functionally either -- partners names are on the title		N	N
Joint Tenancy	Functionally either -- partners names are on the title		N	Maybe
Limited Liability Corporation	Functionally either -- LLC holds title		N	Y
Home Owners Association	Y	N	Y	With wait list
Housing Cooperative	Y	Y	Y	Y
Land Trusts	Y	Y	Y	Y
Nonprofit	Y	Y	Y	Y
Apostolic Association	N	Y	Y	Y

* Affordability rating is about whata is possible with greatest ease, not necessarily what your project would ma▸

** TIC and JT aren't technically separate legal entities on their own so they don't get taxed.

*** "Depends" means you can structure it in a variety of ways.

TRAITS OF LEGAL STRUCTURES

Can heirs inherit?	Familiarity for Professionals & Banks	Equity Building	Taxes Filed	Affordablility Rating (5 is most afforable)*	Ease to Create Rating (5 is easiest)
Y	Y	Y	N/A**	Depends***	5
N	Y	Y	N/A**	Depends***	5
"Economic Interest" is inheritable	Y	Flexible	Pass through to members	Depends***	5
Y	Y	Y	Corporate	1	4
Depends***	Some	Depends on type	Y	3	3
Depends***	Some	Depends***	Y	3	1
N	Y	N	Y	4	1
N	Few	N	Pass through to members	5	1

Permanent Real Estate Cooperatives

The following is excerpted from the Sustainable Economies Law Center website.[96] I'm sharing it because they do a better job than I could of articulating what this model is all about. I consider this to be one of the most important cutting edges of hacking the legal system for cooperative endeavors.

The Vision

A PREC simultaneously decommodifies land, enables community control for structurally excluded communities, and disrupts root causes of racialized inequality. Unlike a conventional housing cooperative, which is formed to provide housing to a defined group of residents, a PREC could be described as a "movement cooperative," because it is designed to provide housing, build a large membership base, and serve members' collective goal to transform our neighborhoods and our systems of finance and land ownership.

Our vision is for a typical PREC to have hundreds or thousands of members who look around at the land and buildings in their community and think: "We should own this!" Rather than watching the fate of their communities be determined by wealthy speculators, large companies, and absentee landlords, PREC members will build collective power, pools of capital, skills, and organized communities that can take action to shape the future of local land and buildings.

In 2017, the Law Center helped officially incorporate the East Bay Permanent Real Estate Cooperative in collaboration with the People of Color Sustainable Housing Network, a community of over 1000 people of color interested in building intentional, healthy, collective, and affordable housing communities in the Bay Area and beyond.

How are PRECs different from Community Land Trusts (CLTs)?

CLTs and PRECs have many similarities and emerge from the same movement toward equitable and democratic control of land. Both engage community members in governance and permanently remove real estate from the speculative market. A primary difference is that most CLTs are 501(c)(3) nonprofits. The cooperative structure of PRECs create promising opportunities:

- Cooperative corporations have the flexibility to take capital in multiple forms, meaning that financing options are greatly expanded.

---

96   Learn more here: https://www.theselc.org/eb_prec_incubation.

- Unlike 501(c)(3)s, cooperatives are not constrained to providing housing to low- and moderate-income people. PRECs can spread the expectation that everyone – high- and low-income – should stop profiting from property and live in price-stabilized housing.
- Cooperatives are platforms for mutual aid and self-help, not charitable assistance. Charities can sometimes create a disempowering divide between the helpers and the helped. The cooperative structure transforms the relationship to create empowered groups of people working together to provide for their own
- long-term housing needs.

Exercise 16: Getting Ready to Choose a Legal Structure

Contemplate on your own and then, when you feel ready, talk and help each other think about questions:

- Would your community vision be best served by private ownership of homes or collective ownership? Why?
- What questions do you need answered **by the core group** in order to make decisions about your legal structure and economic structures?
- What questions do you need answered **by a professional** (lawyer, accountant, real estate agent, etc.) in order to make good decisions?

The community's ongoing need for legal information and resources

This chapter opened by mentioning the complex and sometimes intimidating world of laws and legal structures that intentional communities face. The substance of the chapter was on forming legal structures to allow for and reflect the way your community wants to collectively (and individually) own property. But there are many other legal considerations:

- What labor and employment laws will interact with your collective work practices on the property?
- How will individual and joint liability be handled if things are damaged or people are injured in the community? How can you best manage risks and hazards on the property?
- How can you make sure the agreements and covenants you make together are understandable and do what you want them to do?

- If your community enters into a business or resource relationship with other communities, private businesses, or organizations, how can you best protect your community's interests?
- How will you deal with hostile, dangerous, or illegal behavior in your community? How will you handle visits from law enforcement?
- What can you do to make sure your on-site businesses comply with laws and regulations?

And the list goes on. But you don't need to be a lawyer or hire a full-time attorney to always be there in the community with you. There are tons of resources promoting basic legal vocabulary, forms, and procedures non-lawyers can use, and contact information for legal professionals who can help you when you can't do it on your own.

CHAPTER 11: LAND AND THE IMPORTANCE OF SEARCH CRITERIA

> "Stewarding our own land, growing our own food, educating our own youth, participating in our own healthcare and justice systems, this is the source of real power and dignity."
>
> — Leah Penniman, *Farming While Black*

Land is not just the spot your community sits on. Land holds both history and potential, and is not only a source of security, but also the stage your community plays out their dramas on. Land has inherent worth in a way that little else does — life giving food and water can spring from land, as can material wealth that empowers and grounds communities.

The modern world of real estate obfuscates much of this truth. It treats land as a commodity only, something to be consumed, bought and sold, used, and all too often used up. In a world where zoom meetings have become the norm, we are often not even meeting each other in physical space any more, and this (for all of its goodness in terms of accessibility and low carbon work options) has further disconnected relationships from *place*.

Community provides us with an opportunity to re-invest in a direct relationship with the land. While this is easier to see in rural places where "acreage" is part of the real estate listings many of us will end up pouring through to find "our place," it is also true in urban areas. The most satisfying community experiences I've had have been in communities who know something of the history of the place they are occupying, and have a developed narrative about what that means.

Decolonization and Community Building

One of the early inquiries in this book was about how we can ethically build community on stolen land. The Land Back movement is worth discussing here, even briefly. Land Back, like all movements, is diverse in its tactics and specific asks. The general idea though is that the relationship we currently have with land is one based in oppressive and often violent power dynamics that have been at play the whole time white people have been on this continent, and that it began with the forcible taking of land and claiming it as a possession.

"colonized minds

hear

'ours'

and think of

possession

decolonizing minds

hear

'ours'

and feel

connection"

-- poem by josie

valadez fraire

Sustainability, resilience in the face of change, and living ethical lives all ultimately require a change in this most fundamental relationship. The land — the earth — is literally what gives us life and makes everything we do possible.

I know Land Back advocates who are literally asking that land be returned to the Indigenous tribes who are local to the place. I also know Land Back advocates who are challenging the relationship that people have to the land they occupy, regardless of formal legal ownership.

Here are just a few examples of how communities can change their relationship to land and thus begin the process of decolonization.[97]

• Learning about and celebrating land- and seasonal-based holidays (like Solstices and Equinoxes). This can help begin a practice of not taking land and the gifts — which vary seasonally — for granted, a core piece of starting to change how we relate to land and move toward right relationship.

• Listening for and acting on what is wanted and needed by the land. One method for learning to listen is to use permaculture. Permaculture principles are, according to many Indigenous teachers, simply repackaged Indigenous wisdom and observations. Practicing permaculture with direct acknowledgement of its roots is one way to begin decolonizing.

• If permaculture is too heady or feels overwhelming to learn, you can also get into a practice of sitting quietly on the land and simply listening and observing. Get to know the contours of your land, the plants that grow there, the flows of water and wind. And let what you learn influence your decision-making.

• Having land owned collectively, rather than by (an) individual(s), and thus leaning into feeling connection more than thinking about possession (as the poem that opened this section says).

• Pay "Real Rent" if your local tribes have an established program, or if they don't, reach out and ask how your group can make a monthly donation with this intention. Build into your community budget a line item, and commit to paying it over the long term. Real Rent Duwamish suggests $18.55/person/month (recognizing the Treaty of 1855).

---

97   For more information, see: https://briarpatchmagazine.com/articles/view/four-case-studies-land-back-in-action.

- Finally, literally give land back. If you can afford 75 acres or someone in your group has inherited a 125 acre family farm, and you only need 15 acres for your vision, contact your local tribe(s) and open a conversation about ceding the rest back to them. Or ask them what they want to see happen with it, and be open to ceding not just property rights but at least some control over what your group is doing with the property. Or see if there is a local land trust that is part of the Land Back movement or indigenous-led, and work to put part or all of your property into that trust.

In a decolonized world, a community's relationship with the land is just that: *a relationship*. As Robin Wall Kimmerer (an enrolled member of the Citizen Potawatomi Nation) says in her book, *Braiding Sweetgrass*: "Knowing you love the earth changes you. It activates your will to defend, protect and celebrate. But when we feel the earth loves us in return, the feeling transforms the relationship from a one-way street to a sacred bond. You do not want to harm what loves you. The ultimate reciprocity; loving and being loved in return."

Community is a great place to work on changing ourselves and our worldviews. I encourage groups to consider this core relationship between people and land as one of the more powerful transformations available to us on this journey.

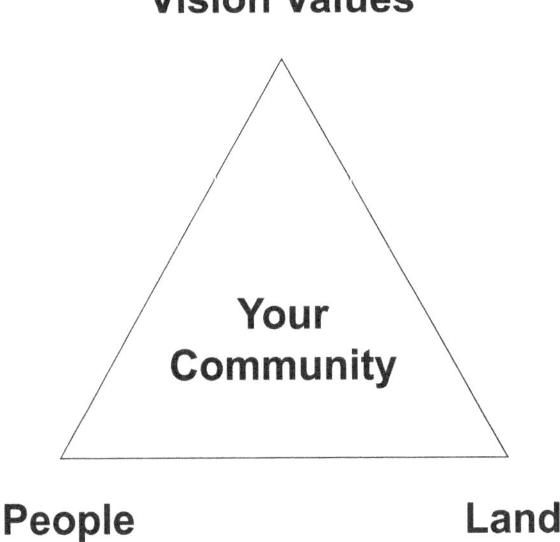

The land and buildings are partners with your people in determining the nature of your community.

Be as discerning about the land and how it fits with your vision as you have been about decision-making and membership.

Property search and acquisition

For many of us, the property search phase is a combination of exhilarating, stressful, inspiring, and overwhelming. Here's my guide for how to have this part be more manageable, and also end up with a property that really works well for your group.

Note that this chapter comes quite late in the book. That's because you have a lot of work to do before you get to this phase. It is especially important to create ownership and membership models, including entry and exit plans, based on your vision. That work will then feed into answering the search criteria questions in a much more coherent way. If property suddenly appears that is a great match, you want to have these things in place before a bunch of money needs to be put on the table to buy it.

Have a business plan *before* you start the search and **more than** enough solid commitments to make it real. (See Chapter 9 for more on what I mean by a business plan.) Watch the market for a while to get a feel for what kinds of things come more and less frequently available where you want to settle. Be prepared with your budget documents to run new scenarios before you make an offer, and adjust your estimated financial needs based on what you learn from watching the market. If you already have a well developed spreadsheet based on the business planning section guidance, you will have a tool handy to understand, for instance, what accepting a counter-offer from the seller might mean for your membership dues or other ways you are planning to get the bills paid.

Work with a real estate agent who can competently partner with you. You may need to educate someone about what communities like yours are and how this is different from a standard transaction. Cassandra Ferrera's workshop on property acquisition for communities could be a great thing to steer them toward if they are willing to take the time to watch it.

The most important new piece of work for your group in this chapter is to create search criteria, based on your vision, ideally before your search begins. I've developed a list of questions that have worked well for the property search for both my own communities and clients I've worked with. I'm sharing that list. Using these questions as a guide, work up a list of property search criteria as a group.

The list will be most useful as a decision-making guide if you prioritize it. At the least, talk about which ones are "must haves" versus "ideally we will have." Note: some criteria may have levels to them, such as proximity to a city, where "within an hour of an urban center" might be a must have, and "within 20 minutes of an urban center" might be your actual ideal. The more thoughtful your group is with this process, the more you will have clear criteria to sort out your options when a property or properties present themselves.

I strongly recommend doing this as pre-search work. There are two scenarios that make this pre-work essential:

1. If a property that some or all of you think has promise suddenly pops up in a fast moving market, you may have to move very quickly. Your group needs a way to either act decisively while staying aligned in that moment, or to be able to resist the temptation to jump on something you may regret a year later. Having well-developed search criteria gives you a way to stay grounded in this moment.

2. You may be in a market with lots of potential options (most commonly for urban groups). In that case, having clear, already agreed upon criteria can keep you from devolving into a battle of personal preferences. Let the mission and values guide these conversations!

Property Search Criteria Questions[98]

1. Do you already have a location picked out or property in hand?[99]
   If not: what states, municipalities, and counties interest you?

2. Have you already looked into legal limitations or benefits in those places?
   If not: What do you need to consider? (Some examples: legalized marijuana, tiny house or composting toilet restrictions, property tax rates, Medicaid expansion, etc.)

3. How urban or rural do you want to be? How near to a major city do you want or need to be? What cultural, social, or economic features does that city need to have? (Some examples: living wage laws, a vibrant arts scene, a particular type of political organizing, etc.)

4. How should your property relate to transportation systems? Close to a major highway, airport, or train station? Walkable and bikeable to amenities?

5. How many people will your ideal community have that the land needs to accommodate? How much land do you ideally want for that to work well? Are there minimum acreage needs for this to be a viable project?

---

98   You can find these questions as a downloadable pdf at: http://www.ic.org/building-belonging-resources

99   If the answer is "yes" to this, some of the questions that follow will serve more as taking stock of what is rather than creating criteria for what you want.

6. Do you want existing structures? If so, what kind? If you want raw land, are there utilities that need to already be in place (like city water or a well, internet cable, an electric grid hook up available for the site)?

7. What water needs do you have and what are the most common water sources and processing options in the area where you are looking? Is there city water and sewage service available, or is it more common to have well water and septic where you are looking? Are constructed wetlands appealing and allowed? Whatever the anticipated water source, is there water test data available for it?

8. What physical features or amenities interest you to have access to (examples: trees, water, parks, next to national forests, mountains, library, jobs, highway, public transit, high speed internet)? For each amenity, consider: Does it need to be on the property? Within an easy walk or bike? Within an easy drive?

9. Are there particular things you *don't* want? (Some examples: heavy winds, openly homophobic neighbors, highway noise, near a confined animal feeding lot, etc.)

10. Do you need zoning that allows for multi-family units? For mixed use functions? How much bandwidth does your group have for getting exemptions if need be? If exemptions might be needed, what body approves those and what is their general orientation?

11. Do you need building codes that allow for certain types of building materials or techniques? If you aren't able to find a place that currently allows what you want, are you willing and able to compromise on materials, location, or the timeline (the latter of which would give you time to seek exemptions or change local policy)?

12. Are there spiritual or ethical considerations?[100] (Some examples: connection to land spirits, Indigenous land history, land reclamation or brownfield development, to not participate in gentrification, etc.)

13. Do you want to grow food, and if so, what criteria will allow for that? How much support (if any) do you need in learning and is there reasonable support for that locally?

14. What factors related to climate disruption are you considering? What are the predictions for this area, and what would you need to build into your plans to prepare for those changes?

---

100 Cassandra Ferrera teaches an excellent course on land relationships and acquisition for communities that covers this topic really beautifully.

15. Are there any existing intentional communities near where you are looking, and are they interested in supporting you?

16. Who do you want to attract as members? Will they mostly come from the local area or from people moving to join you? What do you need to consider in terms of that answer?

17. Are there development ideals you are willing to give up to make it economically accessible to more people? If so, which answers that you've already provided in earlier questions are places you are willing to flex?

18. Are there professionals (in real estate, legal and financial services, design and building, group process and training, etc. in the area(s) you are look ing who are aligned with your community values?

19. Are there any other specific needs you have for your vision?

A few specific thoughts on location:

Costs: coastal communities and liberal cities tend to be more expensive, but have more social services available. The cost to get in might be a bit in tension with the cost of surviving and thriving in a place for the people you want to create community with.

Politics: There is always a good news/bad news aspect to this. Not having hostility is good, but places with less good political alignment may be places that have more need for a project like yours.

Urban versus rural: Urban areas tend to have better access to good jobs, reliable internet, and more racial and cultural diversity, but they also come with lots of distractions (meaning you might have challenges with getting people to focus on the community, both during the start up phase and once you have landed). They are also almost always more expensive.

Proximity to resources: This could be a subset of the urban, rural conversation, except that there are definitely pockets of more progressive and well-funded small towns. Looking for places that have what you need in terms of amenities such as hospitals, water, "alternative" culture, nature, and public transit.

Climate (and the fact that it is changing): Many communities look for places with abundant water, a long growing season, and good soil. Increasingly, it is important to take into account climate disruption impacts that are expected and already happening where you want to locate: sea level rise, unpredictable weather, etc. There are projections available for many places about what may happen in different states, but these are changing as new data emerges.

Still, it can be worth finding out what scientists currently think may happen in the area you are considering in 20–50 years, and at a minimum check current flood zone maps to get a sense of the current baseline. And in a more big picture way, talking about how you are going to relate to changes (both in data and in real time and space).

History of the place: While I've already mentioned the history in the context of Land Back, there are many ways that a place's history might matter. Red-lining and green-zoning practices (both of what are easily google-able if those are unfamiliar terms for you) have created still-existing pockets of racial and class segregation that affect everything from cost of living to quality of public schools to general neighborhood vibes and who has political power in different places.

There are also places with interesting communal or political histories, including Fairhope Alabama, Astoria Oregon, Taos New Mexico, and Yellow Springs Ohio to name just a few disparate small towns that represent interesting pockets of activity in unexpected places. Learning a little about potential places can be fun and lead to some interesting additional factors for you to take into account. Sometimes a place ends up just feeling right because of history that has ripples into the now.

Cost, Codes, and Zoning

Intentional communities are not islands — we are communities embedded in larger communities. These go by a lot of names — everything from the Indigenous tribes whose land we are on, to political environments, to municipalities. And some of those other communities have definite ideas about what should and shouldn't be happening in their space, and the power to legislate around them.

Building codes and zoning are one of the more impactful expressions of those wider community values. They are also two of the three biggest factors in determining how hard or easy it is to get the community you want. They affect affordability, how experimental your project can be, and what kind of self-determinism the community has in terms of the physical plane. (The third factor is property prices, which is pretty self-explanatory.)

Here's a bit about codes and zoning. First, the difference between the two:

Building codes are basically about HOW you can build, and mostly regulate the materials, and quality and safety standards of building projects. Codes are intended to be public safety regulations at their core, and that's a great intention.[101] They also unfortunately are often very limiting for groups wanting to be more experimental or use non-manufactured materials (such as straw bales).

Zoning is basically about WHAT and WHERE you can build, and they limit the type, size, and number of buildings a property can have, and whether the property is used for business, agricultural, or housing purposes. There is usually what is called a "mixed use" zoning option that allows you to combine these purposes. Zoning plays a major role in regulating the so-called "character" of neighborhoods, and mostly serves to reinforce class separations in building patterns and protect property values.

You **must** check the zoning of property you are considering buying to make sure you really can do a community on them, and that might involve a call to the county to confirm it. If you don't have time to do that before an offer needs to be made on a property, I recommend writing confirmation of zoning into your offer as a contingency, which will buy you some time.

Rural Missouri, Tennessee, Virginia, and New Mexico all have lots of intentional communities compared to their population sizes. They have the magic combination of low cost, low regulations, and good growing seasons that have attracted a lot of community founders over the years. That also means that there is potential for being part of a local network that has already navigated the state's culture and regulations. You can spend some time browsing the communities directory maps[102] to see these hot spots.

"Hot spots" means in part that you may be able to find a community mentor in one of those places (as well as more populated places: Boston, Austin, Chicago, and the Bay Area in California, for instance all have much more predictably dense community settlements). Some of the better known and more successful communities took off and became stable quickly because of this mentorship relationship. I encourage all the communities I work with to find the Twin Oaks to your Acorn, or the Sandhill Farm to your Dancing Rabbit Ecovillage.

---

101 In fact, it's such a good intention that if you end up in a place without external codes, it is a good idea to spend a little time creating some internal community codes to make sure buildings don't fall down and kill anyone. For instance, plenty of non-code approved materials have data about them to support the idea that they can be just as safe and structurally sound, but you will need to do some of your own investigations on that if you want to use those materials. Straw bale and cob, for instance, are both **more** fire-safe and earthquake-safe than the most common stick building methods if you do it properly.

102 https://www.ic.org/directory/maps/.

Working for Reform, and Exemptions

"A no is just an uneducated yes."

That's one of my favorite quotes from Brandy McPherson, one of the founding members of O.U.R. Ecovillage in British Columbia. BC is one of the few places where ground-breaking work has been done on "ecovillage zoning" and Brandy's community has led that work.[103] It didn't start with wide scale reform attempts, however. It started with working with their local officials to patiently educate them on how the new building technologies that a lot of communities are drawn to was a reasonable and even positive way to fulfill the intent of building codes, and how intentional village design had enough going for it that should be respected and codified in the form of new zoning designations.

They got there in large part because of persistence, and a willingness to see local officials as potential allies in need of some education (thus the quote) rather than seeing them as enemies or barriers to be overcome. In part because of their work, Canada, in general, is much more receptive than the US. That said, many other communities over the years have faced a similar challenge of being committed to building community in a particular place and needing to dig in to long term work with local officials to make that possible.

The legal and economic contexts that communities form in matters. I got on this soapbox for a whole chapter in *Together Resilient*, and I won't reiterate the whole thing here. I do want to celebrate the places where reform is in the works or has in recent years made community living easier.

Like Boulder CO, where a dedicated group of community activists finally got a cooperative housing ordinance[104] passed in 2017. That ordinance has already impacted affordable housing access in a very expensive urban area. Or the work the Sustainable Economies Law Center has done to pioneer new models for community living, including the Permanent Real Estate Cooperative (you may remember them from the sidebar in the last chapter), inspiring anti-gentrification action with ideas like "Land Without Landlords" and "restorative economics." Or the ongoing work of the Green Building Council, whose website has a whole section for articles on advocacy and policy.[105]

I know many people in the communities movement who have worked for years on reform. It feels important to at least mention in this context that change is possible, both

---

103 Learn more at https://ourecovillage.org/our-rezoning-work/.

104 https://bouldercolorado.gov/services/co-op-housing.

105 https://www.usgbc.org/articles?Channels=[%22Advocacy+and+policy%22].

in the form of getting exemptions to do your project the way you want to, but also to clear the way for it being easier for everyone who comes after us because we worked for larger scale reform.

A real question for your group is whether or not you want to sign up for that work and are willing to potentially delay manifesting all or part of your vision to do it. As you are contemplating where you want to end up, your patience level (and the additional resources it would take to be patient) with the reform process may or may not end up being a factor.

Exercise 17: Develop Property Search Criteria

Using the list of 19 questions from earlier in the chapter, work together as a group to come to your collective answers. Then, prioritize them. What are your "must haves"? What are the top three places where you feel flexible? If it is a choice between affordability and some of your criteria, what are you committing to choose?

You can also find the questions at http://www.ic.org/building-belonging-resources in a printable pdf form.

CHAPTER 12: SOME BASICS OF COMMUNITY DESIGN

I'm neither an architect nor a permaculture designer nor (much of) a builder. So take what I'm saying here with some grains of salt. Recognize that I'm offering observations about what works well, based on having visited over 100 communities and spent enough time in a few dozen to understand what they like and don't like about their space. And I have paid attention to the architects and permaculturalists in my life when they've taught workshops or spoken about their work.[106]

I encourage all groups who are going to hire professionals (architects, landscape planners, builders, etc.) to hire people who have worked with community groups before. There are a whole lot of assumptions that you will want to make as a group doing something collective that runs counter to standard cultural assumptions in the building and design industries.

Fortunately, the communities movement now has a healthy group of architects and builders you can call on. I've also found permaculture designers to be an excellent match for community site planning — they are fundamentally oriented toward seeing humans, the elements, the land, and the weather as a whole system functioning together, and that can lead to labor saving and vibrant site plans.

About the Common House

It is very hard to build community without some kind of shared meeting and eating place. I've seen communities do well with a single, large room and a good supply of tables and chairs that people bring food to for potluck meals. I've also seen groups do well with elaborate, 7,000+ square foot common houses with kids room, full commercial kitchen, guest and office spaces, smaller hangout rooms, laundry, a woodshop. and game room . . . really the sky's the limit on what we can dream up and want in spaces and some groups even have the material resources to manifest them.

Most groups settle for a middle ground — a great room with a kitchen, and a few other spaces that support the kind of community they want to be. In some of the more communal groups, the common house can also provide showers and laundry so that personal spaces do not need to have running water (one of the biggest expenses). In some cases, there are multiple common buildings that serve different needs, or (in

---

106 I've also spent time studying *A Pattern Language* by Christopher Alexander, Sara Ishikawa, Murray Silverstein, Max Jacobson, Ingrid Fiksdahl-King, and Shlomo Angel. This book is an accessible wealth of knowledge about patterns in good design, and I think should be on every community's bookshelf.

larger, more geographically dispersed site plans) different regions of the community that each have their own communal buildings. As I've said elsewhere, these decisions should be guided by your vision and values.

What I don't recommend is not having any shared spaces. Think of it this way: you shape spaces, but then the spaces shape you. If we aren't prioritizing communal functions in the spaces we are building, it is going to be very uphill to create a communal experience. Pulling an example from my cohousing clients over the years, I see a strong correlation between how often groups eat together and otherwise use the common house for collective gatherings, and how well the community is bonded and aligned. That bonding and alignment in turn has a lot of ripples into how well they navigate conflict, and how easily they make decisions together.

I also recommend that you build your common house (or a big-ish common space) early in the building process, and build it to work for common meal sharing. This allows people who don't yet live there to spend time on the property, lets you start meal sharing as soon as it is built (and approved for use), and get all of the bonding benefits of breaking bread together. It also creates a critical psychic draw toward *community* rather than just people's personal spaces.

Site planners also recommend having the common house sited so that folks have roughly equal ease of access to it. This may mean putting it roughly in the center of your planned human habitation zone on the property, or may mean that the common house is between the parking lot and the rest of the community, so folks are encouraged to walk through it on their way home. It is obviously fine to prioritize disability access in the planning; however, be wary of also creating a more-money-means-better-access bias, meaning don't put the bigger fancier houses closer to the common house and a shorter walk to the parking lot.

I attended a common house design workshop many years ago with Charles Durrett.[107] One of the tidbits that has stuck with me was him saying that the most used 20 square feet of the commons in cohousing is the intersection between kitchen and dining room. Picture someone cooking a community meal and others hanging out and talking to them. That casual hanging out while getting the work of community done is like grease in the wheels of all of your relationships. It is also a key place to think through. Picture a line of people waiting in line for a meal, and design for those 20 minutes it takes everyone to get a plate. So if you are going to invest extra money anywhere, I'd recommend doing it there. How well you design that intersection will create either years of ease or years of irritation for your group.

---

107 Charles and Katie McCamant brought the cohousing model to the US from Denmark, and between the two of them, they've designed dozens of cohousing communities in the US.

About Personal Spaces

Everybody needs their own space in community. Even the most extroverted of people need downtime and away-from-people time. We also all deserve to be able to create something that suits our aesthetic and organizing orientation without anyone else getting a say in it. Personal space is incredibly important in community.

How much personal space is something that should tie back into your vision and values. Some communities are designed and structured so that everyone (or each family unit) has their own fully featured and functional personal home. That's the traditional cohousing model, but has also been used for many other communities before cohousing became a codified thing. That choice is easy for most folks to wrap their heads around and is also often an easier entry ramp into community for folks raised on the American Dream mythos than groups less focused on personal rights. It is also resource intensive and expensive, and has implications for both your community's ecological footprint, and its economic accessibility.

Other communities make sure each adult (and child over a certain age) has their own bedroom. If folks decide to communalize their bedrooms, they get to do that (such as a couple deciding to use one of their rooms as the sleep room and one of their rooms as the hangout or work room), but what the community commits to is providing access to a room of one's own.

Both of these models can work, and many communities are somewhere between — everyone has their own space that could be a bedroom in a coop house with all the amenities, a small cabin that meets some needs while the common facilities meet others, or homes that are more minimally featured. There is a big trade off between affordability and lots of personal space — basically the more functions you can communalize (laundry, guest spaces, space big enough to host a party, etc.) the more affordable housing will be.

De-emphasizing large and custom-built personal spaces is going to rub a lot of us westerners the wrong way. People fear getting swallowed up by the group even when they are drawn to community. Making sure personal spaces are guaranteed can help some, but this is one of those places where the group really needs to ask early on how much culture shift you are willing to do. My general advice is to communalize as much as you think you can stand, and then push it just a little further.[108] As people acclimate to living in community, they will often relax about needing to protect themselves and

---

108 Thanks to my FIC companions and especially Sky Blue for helping me find the words for this years ago during a late night hangout session at Twin Oaks.

their family's personal interests. Overbuilding is expensive, so try to plan for more community space as your default.

Some Things to Consider Overall

Materials matter a lot for ecological goals, accessibility goals, and your finances. We might adore imported Italian marble, want things to be approved and built fast, or want our cousin involved in the building with techniques and materials they are familiar with . . . but each of those urges have deep implications for who will be able to live comfortably in your community.

Modern building materials are often toxic, and people with any kind of chemical sensitivities will be automatically shut out if you don't do some discernment about materials. On the other hand, my beloved straw bale and cob house that I built at Dancing Rabbit Ecovillage had enough ambient mold in it during the humid summers that some friends couldn't come over and hang out. That also points to matching materials to your climate, and being willing to ask if a favorite material is a good choice for the heat, cold, humidity. and wind levels of your chosen place.

As a general rule, materials that can be locally sourced and are less manufactured tend to have lower carbon footprints. Natural building materials are also a joy to work with and create amazing spaces to live in. They are also labor intensive to build and if everyone in your community needs to build their own homes, that is going to create a barrier for folks with physical disabilities. The manufactured home industry has taken huge leaps in recent years in coming up with modular options that are both low toxicity and affordable.

In other words, there's a lot to think about. I strongly encourage you to not just default on these questions, but to (again) reference the materials you are using to your vision and values. This is also a great place to ask, "Who or what does this choice privilege?" Everything you choose here is going to work well for some folks and not others, and if you are going to be a community that embodies justice and equity, you need to have authentic conversations about this and then be real about the impacts your choices will have on who can afford to live in your community — both economically and physically.

The second thing I'd urge you to think about is how much you want to be a full life cycle community. In other words, can someone be born in the community, grow up, have their own kids (or not), age in place, and die there? Or are you really just going to be a community that works well for singles, or young families, or people over 55 whose kids have left home?

If you want to be a full life cycle group, you are going to have to build that into your design. That means having a variety of housing options, building in kid-friendly spaces, and making physical accessibility a design priority. Think through scenarios. What if someone with an upstairs bedroom breaks their leg? Is there space they can temporarily occupy? What if a family outgrows their small unit? How hard is it for them to relocate within the community, and will there be some housing that could accommodate, say, a family of seven?

You don't have to go overboard with far-fetched what-abouts. But it is wise to put some attention on common likely scenarios and make sure you are designing so that it works as people's life circumstances change. (There is an added social benefit to that, which is that groups with options tend to retain members longer, leading to more stability over time.)

Some Site Design Basics

Again, take into account that I'm not a professional in this part of the community starting equation. But here's some observations based on years of paying attention and being part of building a few projects out.

Design for people not cars. One of the most consistently satisfying design elements for community site plans is de-emphasizing cars and emphasizing walking and play. Almost all groups need to think about how cars will relate to the site, but think about how to reduce their impact on the people. For instance, you can keep cars at the edges and make paths wide enough for a garden cart to haul stuff to homes. That has the added bonus of being good for folks in wheelchairs and who use walkers, assuming paths to critical locations are paved and even. You still need to plan for emergency vehicle access, but put some real thought into whether everyone really needs their car to come right to their doors. When we design with and for people, it leads to safer places for kids, elders, and pets, and more ability to hear nature doing her thing outside of our windows.

Use natural resources wisely. Systems are a lot more efficient (in terms of natural resource use and labor needed to maintain them) when you don't fight natural flows. Do site design based on what the water, wind, and sun do naturally on the property. This requires some time spent observing and getting to know your property, but it is worth it in the end.

Embrace the permaculture concept of "zones." In a very simplistic nutshell, this means those things that need attention every day should be placed closest to the center of the design; those things that rarely need attention should be furthest out. This may mean things like planting fragile annuals and herbs closer to the common house, and putting an orchard on the edges of the community.

Design to support both public and private time. One of the most useful design principles from *A Pattern Language* is thinking in terms of layers from fully public to fully private. Some spaces, like a courtyard and the common house, are fully public. Some spaces, like your bedroom, are fully private. In between are semi-public (a porch on a house facing the courtyard) and semi-private (a homes' living room and kitchen). You can create a much smoother relationship between people getting social time and alone time by designing so these are on a gentle gradient from fully public to semi-public to semi-private to fully private.

So imagine that courtyard (fully public space) with the porches of homes (semi-public) facing the courtyard and the porch door entering the living room or kitchen of the house (semi-private) and the bedroom(s) either upstairs or tucked into the back of the unit (fully private). This kind of design allows people to be the most in control of how much they interact and are seen by their neighbors in a way that, say, having a bedroom with large windows facing out onto the courtyard would not allow for. Being able to be at choice like that helps community life be more sustainable for everyone because everyone needs community time and everyone needs alone time.

Design to foster that casual, spontaneous contact between neighbors. For instance, if you have everyone's mail delivered to the common house and place parking next to the common house, both encourage people to walk through it on the way home, increasing the likelihood and frequency of "chance meetings" between neighbors. I've heard people talk about their evening routine on a Friday after work being a "two beer walk" meaning that they find themselves in multiple conversations with neighbors while they slowly wend their way to their own house, stopping and conversing with friends on the way.

Finally, if you will be hiring outside help, I strongly recommend using designers (and consultants) who know community, or come from educational lineages with a compatible worldview. The difference between a traditionally trained landscape architect and a permaculture designer is huge, for instance. The difference between an architect who has only designed high rise apartment complexes and one who has worked with the balance between public and private that communities need to flourish is just as huge.

Exercise 18: Design guidelines for your community

While your core group (probably) won't be the actual designers, you will need to hand those professionals some guidance to work from. Spend some time creating a starting place for them. Here's some core questions:

- What do you think is going to be the right balance between private and common spaces?
- Are there land use projects you already know you want?
- What would you need to think about to make sure the design works for kids, people who are aging, and people with physical disabilities?
- What excites you the most about your land, and your envisioned housing design?
- As you spend time on the land, are there new ideas that emerge from that more grounded and less heady space?

PART 3:
TRANSITIONING TO COMMUNITY LIFE

CHAPTER 13: WHAT TO DO BEFORE YOU MOVE IN TOGETHER

Establishing an intentional community is a complex journey, and one that is often not linear. You may end up doing some of the steps out of "order" from the way I've talked about it here, and that's fine. However, I want to recommend a few things that you really ought to do prior to moving onto property together.

Vision and common values. Everything else should flow from this, including who gets an invitation to move in and our alignment about why we are here.

How you are making decisions. Most groups need some training from someone experienced in community living plus the particular decision-making system you choose. Once you are living together, the stakes go up. A lot. Knowing who is making what kinds of decisions and how is essential for things to go smoothly.

Your business plan. It's one thing to get onto property; it's quite another to stay there. Business planning (whether you need it for property purchasing or not) is the very practical work of figuring out how to economically sustain the project. There's nothing worse than a bunch of people taking a leap of faith together and then having the whole thing come apart a year or two later because you didn't think through the money.

Legal structure and ownership model. You won't be able to buy property collectively without this. And if you are starting out on property that one person owns, you need to have a way to transfer the property to the collective in place. Having this handled builds trust, and for some folks will be a prerequisite to feeling safe enough to move their lives onto the land.

How you are getting the work done. Moving in together is rightfully an exciting moment! And the very next moment, you will need to start getting things done collectively. Work out the basics of your labor system beforehand so this transition can be smooth and joyful, and not immediately get you into tension with each other. The details of this will be tweaked many times over the years as you learn how to live and work together, but have at least a high level version of your "starter system" queued up before you hit the ground.

Membership Process (including entry and exit processes). Don't let anyone move onto the property without a clear agreement about what their status is. Once someone is physically there, it gets a lot harder to negotiate this status. Many a lawsuit has been born in this moment when unclear expectations were combined with financial investment.

Your commitments to justice, equity, diversity, and belonging. This should be part of the visioning process. But if it wasn't, make sure you take the time for these conversations before you land. This is fundamentally about who you are building the community for, which includes both physical structures and social ones.

Your conflict resolution system. Tension is inevitable, but long standing stuck dynamics are not. Following the "early and often" principle is only possible if you have clear expectations and adequate tools this early. Like your work systems, this will get refined over time, but come prepared for the real human stuff to intensify once you are actually living together. Working out how you expect to handle things ahead of time — and getting some solid training in the tools you choose to use — is setting yourselves up for success. Ideally you have a conflict resolution team of some kind — some group that is staying up on how to use the tools you've chosen to employ for conflict and tensions, and who can help out when things aren't going well.

Core Committee Functions

In addition to a conflict team, there are a few committees that I recommend getting up and running early, and definitely prior to moving in together.

Membership. You want a group that is responsible for managing incoming members, keeping your recruitment materials up to date, and making sure people are getting well-oriented. The first year of living in a new community (especially for people who will be in community for the first time) can be a really intense ride for people. There's a lot of things that are hard to describe to someone, and even harder for them to really understand ahead of time. Make sure you don't just welcome people in and then assume their transition is going OK. Check in, help them get acclimated, know who to approach about what, and work through any unexpected emotions and struggles they may be having. The Membership Team is a great place for all these functions to live.

Process. These are the folks who track *how* things are getting done, and bring the need for new or revised process to the group's attention. They can make sure training is happening in a timely way in the social arena, that your meeting structures are doing what you want them to, and helping facilitators make good plans and problem solve sticky situations.

Steering. This group keeps track of *what* the community is up to. They may or may not also be the agenda planners. If you have chosen a legal structure that requires a board, they might be the steering committee.

Labor. There's a lot of work for even the simplest of community projects and having a group that helps to manage the flow of work is really valuable. They could basically just be work party planners in some groups, or in ones that are income and labor sharing, might actually have major responsibilities for keeping a complex system up and running and making sure labor is going the places where the community needs it to go.

Finance. This team runs parallel to the labor team, managing finances, making sure accounting, tax filing, and annual budget processes are happening, and may actually be the ones who have signing authority on your bank accounts (though sometimes that is in the hands of steering, as a checks and balances effort).

Maintenance. This team makes sure that buildings and equipment are kept in good working order. They might also be the ones hiring contractors when they are needed.

Some resources on delegation

All of these committees should have a clear job description. The most thorough list of things to consider when creating committees still comes from Laird Schaub, and I recommend going to his blog (communityandconsensus.blogpost.com) and reading up on committee mandates and delegation.[109] You may not need all of Laird's recommended detail all of the time, especially if you are a small group and generally feel like things are functioning smoothly, but I'd recommend getting familiar with his recommendations here so that you will have a way to diagnose things yourselves if something starts to feel off in how your committees are operating.

Another well developed model, which I mentioned in Chapter 7 on decision-making, is sociocracy. While I'm neither an avid fan nor a detractor of the model in general, I do think that the systematic approach to delegation and communication is well worth studying and taking inspiration from. You also might find that your project is large and complex enough to consider adopting the whole model. I am a fan of the organization Sociocracy for All[110] as the most grounded and well developed resource for learning.

Finally, I often recommend to groups I work with to take a page from Dancing Rabbit Ecovillage's playbook for delegation and consider adopting their Power Levels system. Because I'm not aware of this existing online anywhere, here's a brief overview of how that system works.

---

109 http://communityandconsensus.blogspot.com/2010/03/consensus-from-soup-to-nuts.html.

110 https://www.sociocracyforall.org/.

Dancing Rabbit's Four Power Levels

This system for delegation lives within a well-developed standard for what is "plenary worthy." (Meaning, in their case, that it needs to come to their village council for full discussion in a public forum; more commonly that term means that it comes to the full group for consensus.) For items that do not make the "plenary worthy" standard, the work can be picked up by a manager or committee who has that responsibility clearly lined out in their job description or committee charter.

Those job descriptions or charter all have a special line in them that describes what "power level" the body has for their work. (Sometimes they have different power levels for different duties, and sometimes the committee or manager just have one power level designation.) There are 4 "power levels" in this system: Propose, Review, Recall, and Decide, numbered respectively 1 through 4.

There is a procedure for each of these, though **Power Level 1 is really simple**: anyone in the organization can propose anything, whether it is directly in their domain of responsibility or not. Proposals generally go best if they are made to or via the appropriate body, but a little bit of creative chaos is also good for you, and you want people to engage, even if it isn't perfect. Proposals made with PL1 can, however, be ignored if no one with either agenda setting or committee authority decides to pick it up.

Power Level 2: Review

An entity with PL2 can send an email to the group with a proposal, often after getting input from the group or consulting with key parties. This starts a two-week comment period, during which concerns can be expressed, changes can be made, and the community as a whole generally gets a chance to consider and buy into the decision.

At the end of the two weeks, if there are no *unresolved* concerns, the proposal becomes a decision of the group, and is just as binding as if the full group had deliberated in a live meeting and come to consensus. However, if significant enough changes happen to a proposal during this 2-week comment period, it is a best practice to restart the two week window with the sending out of the new proposal.

PL2 is the most common PL given out to committees and managers and is by far the most common way for a decision to be made at Dancing Rabbit.

Power Level 3: Recall

This also involves a two-week comment period, and the decision is also finalized at the end of the two weeks, barring unresolved concerns. The difference, however, is that the community can start acting on the decision the moment the proposal is sent out to the group.

Power Level 4: Decide

Power level 4 is a final decision. The full group has power level 4. It is given to managers or committees only very rarely and there has to be a very good reason for doing so. For instance, Dancing Rabbit's Contagious Disease Response Team can declare a quarantine to protect public health, and once the nonprofit started hiring people more frequently, the Executive Director was given PL4 for hiring in part to protect the community from legal challenges with HR information being made public.

I've found this power delegation system to be one of the more elegant ways to manage the relationship between committees and the full group, and it is definitely time saving. It is also a terrific example of the kind of innovation that has come out of the communities movement — when we are able to operate as small bubbles of social experimentation, and are grounded, as I believe Dancing Rabbit is, in a mission to better the world as a fundamental organizing principle, really cool and helpful systems can emerge.

As you enter the part of the founders journey when you step into living your community dreams, I look forward to seeing what your group will contribute to this growing body of practical, cooperative innovations that are coming out of intentional communities every year.

CHAPTER 14: BECOMING A GOOD COMMUNITY MEMBER

Some day, your community will have moved out of the realm of imagination and planning and onto land. Some day, there will be buildings and people, traditions and in-jokes, food and music, and laughter and gardens . . . and these things will come to define the community you've helped to start.

And for many of us who are founder types, that's when the *really* hard part starts. When the thrill of chasing a dream and the striving to create are over and this thing is established, you will then be faced with either heading off to start something new and breaking your own heart in the process, or becoming a maintainer.

Those who stay have to relearn how to be a member of a community, not only a founder.

The good news about this moment is that you can decide now what aspects of community life you want to focus on, and let go of feeling the overarching responsibility for **all the things**. I strongly suggest taking a break from community life, whether that is for a week or a few months. Getting away and reconnecting with yourself is healthy and important at this stage.

Starting a community is really intense, and being a founder can become more than a role — it can become an identity. Once that identity is no longer needed, you are going to have to do some reinvention of yourself. It is also a great moment to take that space so you can come back and do a more objective assessment of what you helped create. Evaluation of what works well and doesn't work well can help you find a good niche for another kind of energy — the reviser.

I've seen some of the most effective founders move into a role of identifying problems (yes, some of which they probably helped create!) and then having the grace to work with others to solve them and make changes to the community systems. I've also seen founders discover new loves and be able to reap the benefits of the community container they helped create — maybe you become a gardener or perfect your community cooking skills or finally organize that library. Or maybe you move into being a mentor-on-call, available as an elder voice in the project when someone seeks you out.

There's a lot of ways to play this moment: my core point here is that it IS a moment, and you get to be deliberate about what role you play moving forward . . . but that only works with some self reflection time. Most communities need to de-center their founders in order to really come into their own. (Some people say the founders have to leave for this to happen, but I don't think that is true. What is true is that how you relate to the community will need to change over time, and everyone will be better off if you can have grace with that.)

You've been creating something that will hopefully outlive you, and that is a remarkable legacy. In the meantime, though, you are a real person who is probably going to have a lot of real and complex feelings about the process and the community itself. Now is an excellent moment to take stock of that, and be as loving with yourself as you can be as you sit with that complexity.

Beware and Be Aware: Founder's Syndrome Is a Thing

Founder's Syndrome is an almost universal experience in any long term organization, and community is no exception to that. It is often tossed out somewhat derisively and communicates an underlying sense of founders being out of touch with their own project or power tripping, but I think it is more nuanced than that. As a founder, part of your transition to becoming a good community member will be navigating the dynamics associated with your role.

This is a real phenomenon that you need to understand, but it does not make you a bad person or a bad leader if it crops up. Here's what I think is happening (based on observing other founders and getting caught in these dynamics myself):

1. Founders have maximum influence and say in how things are set up, and that means that, in the scheme of things, you have more overall power. This is absolutely true, though in the daily life of your community, many years after those initial decisions were made, it might not feel like you are still wielding power and influence. But you are: it's just built into the bones of the project at this point. You will also have had a lot more accumulated say over who is here. That's influence as well.

2. You will always have the longest institutional memory. The trick is to offer things more like a historian than to get caught in a trap where you say "this is just the way it is" and are unwilling to hear new voices or recognize when it needs to change. Things **will** need to change, and you have to stay current on why your old decisions (which may have served the group really well at one time) are still the best decisions, or be willing to demonstrate some flexibility.

3. You know why you did this . . . but not everyone does. This phenomenon opens a lot of space for projection. We humans are storytelling animals, which is one of the beautiful things about us. But we also have a tendency to fill in unknowns, and some folks will not be very generous with questions of motivation. So you might

need to not only communicate what you did, but why you did it — and find a way to do that that is not defensive or self-glorifying.

4. You are highly invested. If you weren't, this place wouldn't exist. But here's the kicker: people *joining* a community don't need to share your "burning soul" drive and healthy obsession. *They can be less invested and still be plenty invested to be good joiners and community members.* That doesn't mean they don't get a voice. Founders can definitely get into a space of not just protectiveness of your project but **over**protectiveness. It's good to be willing to ask yourself if someone having a different relationship to the project is OK and even healthy, and to do the hard work of still treating all current members as real partners. Creating a hierarchy in your head (based on your perception of investment) of whose voices are worth listening to does no one any good and will damage your community in the long run.

5. You will always have worked longer (and probably harder) than anyone else. This is just true. If the community lasts long enough, there will eventually be people there as adult members who were not even born when you were working your ass off to get this thing going. This is just real. But you don't get to use this as currency in communications or decision-making. Your project might have gotten off the ground because you founders were amazing, but it would not *still* exist if *other* people hadn't joined the work. Remind people how amazing you still are through your present-time actions not your particular take on the good old days and it is likely to go a lot better.

6. You are who you are and may well have surrounded yourself with people like you. Being with "my people" is often an urge that gets communities built. However there is a downside: in constructing things for your comfort, you have probably inadvertently shut down some diversity. Someday, someone will want in who would be a fine community member, but is not like you in significant ways. Part of maturing is to learn how to open the door wider. This doesn't mean you were *intentionally* discriminatory (racist, sexist, transphobic, ableist, etc.). But it does mean you have an obligation to change as the times change and as people from more diverse backgrounds want to join the party who may challenge core assumptions you didn't even know you had. Let them, and try to stay present with the process.

7. You are human. In addition to whatever people project on you, you will also genuinely screw up sometimes. And being a founder means two things: you will be there through everything with more chances to screw up than anyone else simply because of this longevity, and you will also have people blame you for structural defects (fairly or not). Getting feedback is hard. Recognizing the ways you have caused damage is hard and, in this case, extra hard for many people because it is

both very public and in a context that is and has always been high stakes for you. (See *The Cooperative Culture Handbook* section on feedback for leaders in Key 13: Hierarchy Lite for some help.)

Finally, one of the best things you can do for your community is to celebrate it. Getting a community off the ground is a huge achievement. By this point, you will know that better than anyone. Take delight in your collective creative powers, even if it is not exactly what you pictured when you started.

CONCLUSION

I feel incredibly fortunate to have found the world of intentional communities relatively young. At 26, I had had just enough time as an adult out in the wider world to know that I wanted something different, but I had no real idea of what that might be.

Being able to step into a community that was fully realized was like stepping into magic: gardens to while away an afternoon in, people to learn from and stay up late getting to know, other parents to help when we had rough baby moments (or hours), woods to get away from all the other people into, food and health security, a huge kitchen to play in . . . it was all there, and I was wide eyed and open hearted, learning to be a communitarian.

Those early community years were some of my most formative ones. Community started working on me right away and made me a better person: more thoughtful, less cynical, more able to believe that my creativity and labor meant something to the people around me. And I can still remember the feeling that came over me sometimes — the shock of bone-deep recognition: THIS was how we learn to be fully human.

Now of course I know something of the years of intense work, debates, choices, and planning that went into getting that community to where it was when I could just join. I know that it wasn't magic, but rather commitment and hard work and frequent heart break.

But I've also heard the stories about the early days of that community, and now I've made a few of my own in different projects. I can say with certainty that this journey is also fun and stimulating, and at moments, even pure joy.

It's easy to lose sight of it some days, and I worry a little that me being real in this book about the overwhelming amount of decisions and work of this journey to start a community might dissuade you from doing this yourself. There is wisdom in the notion that we only do things because we have no idea what we are getting ourselves into, and I'm afraid I may have blown that for some of you.

So I want to leave you with this thought: I've never laughed so frequently as I did with my co-founders. I've never shared as many hugs and in-jokes and evenings of simple companionable pleasure as I did in those years of pulling community together from the threads of our disparate lives.

Community is our birthright. Those parts of our brains that evolved as people living in bands, then tribes, and then small villages are part of our essential nature, regardless of what we were born into. They create a longing in us to do well with other people, to know other people well and be seen, and to get our needs met without having to do every damn thing on our own.

Finding ways to knit together our lives in a time and place of deep separation is not always easy. I'm deeply grateful to all of you who are picking up the mantle of community founding. May your journey be rich and nurturing and inspiring, and may you one day stand in the middle of the commons you helped create and feel deeply satisfied with what you've done together.

APPENDIX LIST OF EXERCISES

APPENDIX LIST OF FIGURES AND CHARTS

www.ingramcontent.com/pod-product-compliance
Lightning Source LLC
Chambersburg PA
CBHW081143130726
47996CB00009B/2957

9 798218 166489